GPS *for the Soul*

WISDOM OF THE MASTER

786
Love & blessings
always, Victoria
Dana

DANA HAYNE

BALBOA
PRESS

A DIVISION OF HAY HOUSE

Balboa Press books may be ordered through booksellers or by contacting:

Balboa Press
A Division of Hay House
1663 Liberty Drive
Bloomington, IN 47403
www.balboapress.com
1 (877) 407-4847

Because of the dynamic nature of the Internet, any web addresses or links contained in this book may have changed since publication and may no longer be valid. The views expressed in this work are solely those of the author and do not necessarily reflect the views of the publisher, and the publisher hereby disclaims any responsibility for them.

The author of this book does not dispense medical advice or prescribe the use of any technique as a form of treatment for physical, emotional, or medical problems without the advice of a physician, either directly or indirectly. The intent of the author is only to offer information of a general nature to help you in your quest for emotional and spiritual well-being. In the event you use any of the information in this book for yourself, which is your constitutional right, the author and the publisher assume no responsibility for your actions.

Any people depicted in stock imagery provided by Thinkstock are models, and such images are being used for illustrative purposes only.
Certain stock imagery © Thinkstock.

Print information available on the last page.

ISBN: 978-1-5043-8404-9 (sc)
ISBN: 978-1-5043-8405-6 (hc)
ISBN: 978-1-5043-8406-3 (e)

Library of Congress Control Number: 2017910663

Balboa Press rev. date: 08/04/2017

Dedication

To all those who have lost their way.

Epigraph

There's no place like home.

—Dorothy, *The Wizard of Oz*

Acknowledgments

I 'd like to acknowledge Rodger, my forever friend, who, for over forty years of marriage, has agreed to be my mirror and who so lovingly provided the safe platform that enabled the writing of this book.

Preface

In November of 1973, I met His Holiness Muhammad Raheem Bawa Muhaiyaddeen,[1] a mystic from Sri Lanka who became what I consider the father of my soul. For the next thirteen years until his passing, I lived and studied along his side at the Bawa Muhaiyaddeen Fellowship in Philadelphia and briefly in Sri Lanka. What follows are vignettes from those years.

Over that span of time, thousands from all religious, social, and ethnic backgrounds joined in his presence to hear him sing spontaneous songs in praise of the divine or to hear him speak about the nature of God and how to achieve the state of man/God and God/man, the ultimate egoless state of self-annihilation. Many who came considered His Holiness an enlightened being. Some from the Sufi tradition believed him to be the *Qutb*,[2] or the

---

[1] *Muhaiyaddeen* (Arabic): One who restores to life the path of purity. The awakener of wisdom that lies hidden in illusion.

[2] *Qutb* (A): The supreme saint of the age; the physical embodiment or manifestation of divine wisdom, which discerns right from wrong; the spiritual axis around which the entire cosmos revolves.

physical embodiment of wisdom, whose mission was to awaken faith and to give life to the truth. Eschewing honorifics himself, this humble man, who referred to himself as an "ant man," spoke in parables and encouraged each of us to see all lives as our own, to acquire God's divine qualities, and to die to the false self or to die before death.

More often he referred to himself as a traffic cop, suggesting that he had been down all the roads, and that his job was to point the shortest way, as some paths could take lifetimes. Always, he urged, the shortest, most direct route to God was through the heart.

My hope is that by sharing these anecdotes perhaps others, who are suffering or feeling lost in this world or who simply want to find *home*, will be touched by the principles taught by this individual, as was I, and will be inspired to study the universal wisdom left behind in his many books and the thousands of hours of video and audio files.

His Holiness M.R. Bawa Muhaiyaddeen

PART ONE

Before

Introduction

When does it start? Life, that is. Existence, being-ness, whatever I call me—when does it start? Where do I start? They tell us at birth, that Hallmark moment, which is carefully penned next to those tiny, inky-black foot prints on one's birth certificate, a moment so hallowed that it is judiciously tallied and memorialized once per annum by each of us, whether publicly or secretively. But no, they've got it all wrong. I'm certain—because I can remember.

When I was three, my family lived on a military installation situated at the mouth of the Panama Canal in the Pacific Ocean. Each afternoon, eager for respite from the tropical sweat and swelter, my young mother put her three little girls down for naps. Not tired, I lay on my bed with Peter Rabbit tucked safely under my chin. As I lay there stroking my friend's ratty and torn ears, it was as though a portal opened and some part of me slipped through to another world. This is where I would commune with *before*.

Poor Peter—the safety he offered paled in comparison to the presence

I found enveloping me. This presence was not populated with things or persons but rather feelings—feelings of safety and contentment. Friendly feelings. There was no stuff to all this. Just feelings and light. Bright light. Sparkly and cool. There were no questions disturbing the stillness, just knowingness. I remember exploring the bounds of this presence and how it felt endless. I remember delighting in the certainty of its endless, joyous nature, which was somehow not separate from me. Somehow, I was this expansion.

Gradually over time, this portal to *before* sealed itself and became a dull memory as those I trusted as older and wiser began to graft branches of ignorance onto the pure rootstock of my being. Each of them carefully stuck sticky notes all over me, as if I needed reminders of who I was:

Spittin' image of your Aunt Francis.

You're good. You're bad.

You're right. You're wrong.

You're thin. You're fat.

You should be a doctor when you grow up.

You're this. You're that.

You. You. You.

Are. Are. Are.

From that Hallmark moment, called birth, parents, teachers, priests, and nuns, took turns molding me. Like some bonsai project, they tweaked my uniqueness, this boundless, endless, being-ness into sameness so that today I stand here looking at my hybrid self, imploring the heavens for the wisdom to cleave these grafts and strip me to my original source, leaving me with the resounding question: who am I?

The nuns and priests in their long, black, foreboding habits worked hard at molding me. Saturday nights I can remember whispering with my two older sisters, bedded down in the same attic room with me, about the dread of confession the next morning. "Come on, guys! Get serious! We gotta go in that box again tomorrow! We gotta come up with something!" We searched hard among our innocent beings to come up with new and noteworthy sins to report, as "arguing with my sisters and brothers" and "disobeying my parents" occurred so frequently that most certainly we were damned for failure to repent. Desperate to keep the box experience to a minimum, I whispered, "Well, guys, I'm going with number seven," as "adultery" was one of the big ten I hadn't yet presented, to which my older sister, Linda, suggested, "Nope, nope, nope! Best to stick with the usuals."

So, sin in hand, I knelt, trembling, in the cold, sterile confessional and waited my sentence from the priest's disembodied voice. "Bless me Father for I have sinned. I did not go to church last Sunday." "This is a grave sin, my child," rumbled the Voice. "You must pray ten *Hail Marys*, ten *Our Fathers* and fifteen *Acts of Contrition*."

Now, that just wasn't fair! I mean really! God went with me everywhere, and we struck up conversations whenever and wherever—bathroom, bedroom, playground. Besides, I thought, it was just too far to walk to church, and Dad was often gone soldiering and not around to take me. As I knelt there reciting my penance, I offered prayers from the heart—confused prayers.

Things didn't improve when the nuns told me that babies, who weren't baptized, went to limbo, a place where they could never know God. This heartless deity didn't sound like the friend I conversed with. No friend of mine would ever condemn these souls to eternal separation or deny them entry into purgatory, should there even be a need for atonement.

I pretty much unsubscribed my membership after a particularly unnerving sermon one Sunday, which further mapped out the rules of admission into heaven, barring all non-Catholics from entry. No way! Good-bye! Sayonara! If my best friend, Mickey, who was Jewish, whatever that was, wasn't allowed in, then I didn't want any part of this group. The veils continued to drop, with me too young to articulate my confusion and to question these edicts set forth by trusted, greater authorities.

Home was a most unsteady foundation. Being a military family, we moved frequently, and by the time I was six, we had relocated six times, eventually settling in a two-bedroom beach cottage, situated steps from the Atlantic in the then-sandy, undeveloped dunes at the north end of Virginia Beach. My naval officer father spent long periods overseas, leaving my highly educated and intellectual lawyer-mom with five small children to raise quite literally by herself, a situation for which all her brilliant book knowledge had not prepared her.

Everyday life at home was most confusing. Some days were spectacular, like being wakened at two in the morning to experience the eye of a hurricane. "Come children, quickly," Mom whispered. "You don't have to get dressed. But hurry or we'll miss our chance." Yawning, hand in hand, we'd stumble after Mom down to the beach, the sand cold and damp between our toes. We'd sit there, jumbled together in our jammies in the sand dunes in the eerie calm and half-light of the storm, and just observe.

I remember the ocean— flat and glassy, with only an occasional, slow ripple. The air was so still it was as though the earth had stopped breathing. But the birds, vast numbers of tiny birds, were everywhere, clinging to the sea oats. Where had they all come from? They clung to their vegetative anchors, without so much as a chirp or a twitter, in contrast to our border collie, Robo, our canine climatologist, who trembled and whimpered at our feet, instinctively aware of the sinking millibars.

Satisfied that we had absorbed the experience, Mom marched us back to our beds and tucked us in, reading to us from Edward Lear's *The Quangle Wangle's Hat*, complete with the voices of the Fimble Fowl and the Quangle Wangle himself.

Other days were like living on top of a highly combustible, well-laid fire, just waiting to be sparked into conflagration, compounded by the drunken screaming matches that ensued every time my father's ship sailed in. At night, my sisters and I would sneak down from our beds. Huddled at the bottom of the steps outside their bedroom door, we'd listen to their frightful rages, feeling somehow culpable for their disharmony, certain that he would leave yet again. He's gonna leave again, I fretted. And it's all my fault. I shouldn't have pulled Karen's hair when she called me a sissy.

I lived very little of my childhood as a child. "Daaaanaaaaa! Set the table! Pour the milk! Feed the dogs! Wash the dishes!" Every night, seven days a week, I jumped to those commands. Middle among five, I had this bizarre notion that my role in life was to save my very overwhelmed mother, so I spent most of my time Cinderella-like at her service.

I recall laundry day, pre-dryers and Pampers, mind you. Standing on tiptoes, just able to reach the clothesline, I'd construct an imaginary castle with elaborate labyrinths and hidden passages out of those many baskets of diapers. Periodically, I'd drop my arms to my sides to ease their bloodless ache and heaviness. Feeling returned, I'd shove my glasses back up my nose, tiptoe again, and resume construction of my cloth castle, pondering whether shirts dried faster if you hung them from their shoulders or from their tails.

Clearly my two older sisters had some other notion of their relationship to this family, as they were off on their own adventures, not to be constrained by chores and usually in open conflict with Mom. Oh, I remember those most frightening "front-and-center" moments when Mom, in a fury, shouted, "Front and center! Attention!" She'd shout at us about messes and homework and undone chores, brandishing her weapon of choice, the fly swatter.

The three of us stood there—Linda, Karen, and Dana—arranged by age and height. Mom would start with Linda, screaming all kinds of threats, the specifics of which I cannot remember because I was just too scared. Like some brazen stallion, Linda was bound and determined not to be broken by this towering wall of rage and would stand there unblinking as Mom lashed her with the fly swatter, crying, "This hurts me more than it hurts you!" That was one declaration I could *never* wrap my head around. How, pray tell, was this hurting her!

Unable to break Linda, Mom would then turn to Karen. Under my breath, I'd whisper, "Karen. Just cry! Just cry and she won't hit you with that *thing!*" However, ignoring my whispered advice, Karen stubbornly took her lashings as well. Not me! No way, José! As soon as I saw Mom raise that disgusting, dirty, germ-ridden thing in my direction, I'd start whimpering, and she'd hold off lashing me. Then abruptly, the whole lot of us women, Mom included, would disband to our separate corners, each crying our own separate tears of frustration. God only knows what was happening with my two younger brothers as we women warred hormonally.

It was so odd the way all the fierce law and order became absurd levity and humor once Mom had a drink. A few fingers of bourbon under her belt and she'd switch gears out of the blue from major general to matador. "Toro! Toro!" she shouted, brandishing her dish cloth matador's cape in front of her. I never knew how to respond to this quixotic lightheartedness and think I quite disappointed her as I stood there motionless, wondering if I should run for safety or continue the charade and drop to all fours and become a charging bull. Either choice, I risked her wrath.

Thank God for the beach with its dunes and rolling waves. They became sanctuary and reprieve from the daily stress and drama at home. When things were at their worst, I'd sneak off and hide among the sea oats, contemplating the contrast between the smooth, glassy curl of the waves breaking below and the erratic tension at home. I'd watch the rhythmical dip and dive of the dolphins and wonder how different and violent man seemed compared to these aquatic creatures, who moved effortlessly in harmony and in sync with each other.

I knew something was dying in me and felt I might just go crazy if I didn't get out. And, boy! I wanted out *big time*! However, as far as I could see, there were only two ways out: marriage (*not*) and education. So I maximized my little brain cells into overachievement and managed a scholarship to Goucher College in Towson, Maryland, then still an all-girls' school.

Unfortunately, I was so absolutely not prepared for the social dynamics of an all-girls' school in the '60s! I remember the first week at school, waiting excitedly in the lobby of the dorm with a bunch of freshmen girls for our ride to our first fraternity party. The flattery I felt for having been among those chosen to attend was squashed pretty quickly when our escorts insisted on blindfolding us for the ride, explaining, "Not to worry. It's a Bonnie and Clyde theme." Worry! Worry didn't even begin to explain the shock when our blindfolds were removed and we stood before a receiving line of tuxedoed young men, trouser-less in their skivvies, not to mention that the non-alcoholic punch was laced with LSD, which meant I spent the remainder of the night on my first acid trip, alone in the lobby of the dorm, freaked out by the loud gurgle of the air-conditioning system.

Add to this the girls: One of my roommates was an exquisitely beautiful Jewish girl from Long Island, who spent her extracurricular time either shoplifting or binging and barfing. Innocently, I wondered where all the new clothes came from and where all the food went. Another roommate confided that she was gay and felt highly threatened by her jealous lover, who, fearful of a rival, planted stolen goods in the rooms of anyone who tried to befriend her lover, and then ratted the supposed thief to the campus police. Yikes!

With the social dynamics so unsettling, I threw myself into my studies, just hoping that scholarly minds had the answers my parents and the church lacked. Carefully, I selected electives in psychology and philosophy.

Perhaps therein lay the truth. But I shook my head at Sartre and his ideas of existentialism and shuddered at the notion of atheism.

Each spring at the end of the school year, I'd eagerly pack up my belongings and head home, keen to escape these most confusing social dynamics, imagining that maybe, just maybe, home would be a safe haven. Silly me. I'd complain bitterly to my mom that I didn't want to go back to school, and of course, I didn't dare tell her squat about all the shenanigans, for ours was not a relationship of intimacies.

You see, Mom was desperate that at least one of her children succeed in the arena of academia. Each time I broached the subject, she'd table the conversation, saying, "Let's discuss this at the end of the summer." This cycle continued for three years until I finally got smart and realized that ironically, failing was the only way to ensure my dismissal. Classes were mandatory, which made failure easy. I basically "hookied" myself into dismissal, then dropped my search for book knowledge and went in search of experience.

First I went to the Virgin Islands, expecting to find paradise in a place. I spent a year as a professional guide, taking tourists through the underwater snorkeling trails at the Buck Island National Park of St. Croix. I was so totally in awe of the natural beauty of the island's flora and fauna. However, I found it exceptionally disturbing that the professionals of the island, doctors, lawyers, accountants twenty and thirty years my senior, were still behaving like adolescents, downing hash brownies and shots of tequila at any time of day. Was this what would become of me if I stayed here, I wondered? Keeping this in mind, I spent the rest of the year sailing, diving, and eating tropical fruits but eventually came home defeated and depressed, not having found what I was looking for. What I had learned, however, was that changes in geography changed little, as you take yourself with you. So, I tucked life lesson number one into my arsenal.

Wherever you are is only as good as the state of your mind.

My next escape tactic was to flee to Israel, where it was possible to live and work on a kibbutz for free. Secretly, I hoped that a stint in the Holy Land might rekindle my faith that had been lost in the confessional cupboard of shame and the torpor of Dad's empty Jack Daniels bottles. Off I went with my toothbrush, backpack, and two pairs of blue jeans. Somehow, I made my way from the Kibbutz Program Center in Tel Aviv to Kibbutz Evron, which was situated just kilometers south of the Lebanese border and across the highway from the medieval, walled, coastal city of Acre. I spent the next twelve months climbing thorny grapefruit trees and hefting seventy-five-pound sacks of bowling ball–sized grapefruits, alongside the most eclectic group of hippie nomads from all over the globe: Japan, Kenya, Australia, Denmark, England—individuals like myself who were looking—looking for something.

As a bonus for all our unpaid labor, the kibbutz organized monthly cultural excursions around the country for its volunteers. This suited me just fine. I thought that surely I could regain my faith in this holiest of holy lands, where so many prophets had walked, where my beloved Jesus had walked. In those ten months, I scaled Masada, waded the Jordan, crossed the Galilee, and genuflected on hallowed ground, unfortunately with no hint of spiritual awakening.

Most significant for me was the Wailing Wall, where I watched the crowds of faceless men, huddled along the length of the massive sandstone wall, faces shielded by tallit and tefflin. As I listened to the low, guttural hum of their whispered prayers, I watched as they carefully shoved tiny scrolls of parchment into chinks in the wall. *Dear God*, I wondered, *do You read these little pieces of paper? Is this true communion?* Disillusioned and disappointed, I left what was for me the Un-Holy Land, with the beginnings of lesson number two starting to filter in.

God is in the heart, not in a place.

Since home had proved an unsafe haven, I went to live with my sister in Woodstock, New York, on top of Bear Mountain in a one-room cabin. I bunked with Cooni-oshi, a baby raccoon rescued from a forest fire. Cooni-oshi, true to his nocturnal nature, kept me awake at night, exploring the depths of my nostrils and the labyrinth of my ear passages with his tiny, soft paws.

Woodstock in the early '70s was an education in itself, a most remarkable "turned on" locale, where it seemed that entry into the pack was predicated on uniqueness. The entire hamlet screamed, "Who are you?" It seemed everyone was a star of something.

Gradually, as I made the transition from kibbutznik, life took on a new rhythm. By day, I waited tables at an Israeli restaurant, called Joshua's Café, to fund my return to school. Nights found me dancing at an aptly named nightclub called the Joyous Lake, a smooth, organic environment of wood, glass, and broad-leafed tropical plants. Stars seemed to burst from the shadows with precious regularity at the Joyous Lake such that on any given night, one might party with the likes of Bob Dylan, Bonnie Raitt, Paul Butterfield, the Band, or Janis Joplin.

Challenging these musical maestros for the limelight were the spiritual superstars, such as Swami Satchidananda and Swami Muktananda, who had descended upon Woodstock during the first wave of the great guru invasion of America. These bearded babas and swamis had much of Woodstock "om-ing" and "ahh-ing" by the time I arrived. For myself, I wasn't particularly impressed or drawn to this movement, which quite honestly, I considered flaky. However, one pivotal weekend, I reluctantly agreed to attend a gathering led by a Harvard graduate, a Mr. Richard Alpert, alias Ram Das. It seems this brilliant mind was recently back from India and after an enlightenment experience was selflessly offering free solutions to human suffering.

I lasted only briefly at said event once I stepped inside the front door. Through clouds of marijuana smoke, I could see female devotees, breasts and nipples visible through their sheer gauze garments, undulating to the frenzied beat of tablas and the high, ear-piercing trill of shehnais. Round and round they spun, circling our host, who sat grinning in the middle of the gathering, eyes heavenward, hands raised in supplication.

I should have known that nothing of value was being peddled at this event because sex and drugs had consistently failed to bring me peace of mind or happiness. But as the music stopped and the room quieted, foolishly, I raised my hand and ventured a question about the purpose of life and reality, part of me hoping, still hoping that someone held the answer to my search. I was surprised and stunned when sharp wit and intellect responded to the innocence of my query. I sat there embarrassed and disappointed, and once the audience stopped tittering, I quietly made my escape.

In hindsight, I have to thank Ram Das for his barbed reply because ultimately, he helped me launch my rocket in the right direction. Oddly enough, it was one of the dancing devas from that fateful night, whom I met in the health food store the following week, who told me about this little man from Sri Lanka in Philadelphia. "Perhaps," she suggested, "you might like to accompany me there."

PART TWO

After

PART TWO

Breaching the Barrier

Meeting His Holiness defined my life into two distinct epochs—
before and *after*. Stepping into his world, it was as though I had shattered the speed of light and burst into a whole new dimension—a new frontier where all the rules were new and where nothing from my past was useful for survival. Somehow I had breached all the cultural rules and boundaries—the sacred ring-pass-not—that family and culture had designed and assiduously hammered into place to keep all of us the *same*. I was on the other side now, and there was no going back—a state, I might add, that was terrifically refreshing as well as terrifying. I'll never forget the power of our first meeting, which took place shortly after my encounter with Ram Das and the dancing devas.

One early predawn morning, my new friend Dotty and I bundled into her battered but trustworthy rusty blue Mustang convertible and dropped down the New York State Thruway to the City of Brotherly Love for me to meet this holy man from Sri Lanka. On arrival, the two of us were ushered into the second-floor kitchen of the fellowship meeting house to wait—for what, I didn't know. While waiting *ages*, we were tea'ed and talked to by one of Bawa's Sri Lankan lady disciples. I watched as Najma, bangles clinking, poured the steamy-hot, spiced tea back and forth from one cup to another in a three-foot foamy cataract, cooling it to "just right." As she poured, she pried.

"Yes, Auntie, I was living in Woodstock."

"Yes, Auntie, I did smoke ganja."

"No, Auntie, I don't know about demons. What do you mean demons can enter people when they take drugs? What do you mean that I might need to be exorcised?" (By now, I was beginning to get scared.)

"Come darling!" she said, "Quickly! Put your tea down. We have to go see him. Now!"

Swooping the tail of her brilliantly colored royal-blue and gold sari over her head like a scarf, Najma took me by the hand and dragged me into Bawa's room. She walked right up to the bed where he sat cross-legged, and she started rattling away to him in what I assumed was Tamil, his native language. I stood there bashful and uncertain, watching, not understanding. As she chortled, I watched.

Oh, indeed, this being in front of me was beautiful! There was no other word for him. His eyes! Vast, creamy pools that reflected the light of universes; the twinkle of constellations stared at me. Those eyes seemed like they could enfold you with the tenderness of the divine mother if your soul cried from its depths—or skewer you like a hawk should you get out of line. Unable to hold his gaze, I looked down and surreptitiously studied his form while Najma continued to babble to him. His limbs were long-muscled, thin, and supple like a reed, and he had long fingers and toes, narrow hips, and broad shoulders. His skin, a deep, nutty brown, stretched without wrinkle over high, high cheekbones above a mirthful, impish mouth with full lips and proverbial, pearly white teeth. What a curious combination of opposites was this being in front of me. On one hand, he appeared birdlike—light-boned, airy, and ethereal—but on the other, he appeared to have the coiled, contracted, ignition-ready energy of a runner awaiting the starting gun. His physical presence seemed incredibly exhilarating yet simultaneously profoundly still and peaceful. It was as though he possessed a deep, palpable silence, even when immensely active.

Suddenly, Najma and Bawa had stopped talking, and I found myself no longer the observer but the observed—for Bawa had turned his attention from Najma to me. From his perch, he beamed at me with the most beatific, penetrating gaze, such that I felt transparent—like glass, and like he could see through me. Standing there under the force of that unimaginable, unconditional love, I knew he could see all the dirt—all the questionable pieces I tried to hide from others so they might love me. But despite seeing all this dirt, he did love me. And for a moment, I felt adored. I felt pure and innocent. For a moment, I felt the bliss of being complete in all my God-given loveliness.

Unfortunately, this bliss was short-lived and I was brought back to the moment when Bawa addressed me in a high-pitched, singsong voice, which Najma translated.

"So, *pullé* [child], why did you take these drugs?"

What? What was he asking? Take the drugs? Well, gee! I didn't know. How would I know? I'd never even thought about why. I just wanted to be in, and it seemed like drugs were part of the admission package.

"And *pullé*, your brother. Why did you give these drugs to your brother?"

Holy shit! My brother! How did he know I had a brother? Why was he asking me about him? How did he know that I had turned him on to drugs? By now my cheeks were burning with embarrassment. What was going on? In thirty seconds, I had gone from bliss to bummed!

Compassionately, Bawa broke our gaze. He motioned me forward, put his hand on my head, and recited what felt and sounded like prayers or a blessing. Then he placed an apple in my two hands, and he gently suggested that I not do that drug thing anymore. The next moment, I was in the kitchen once more with Najma, being tea'ed and chatted to yet again.

After that first meeting, I fell headlong, Alice-down-the-hole into those eyes for the next two decades of my life, where Bawa took me on a mystical journey exploring the nature of reality. To live with Bawa was to live raw and exposed—without artifice, makeup, or smoke screens. Living with Bawa was to learn to love the mirror. I wanted this—this thing that Bawa had, so I moved to be near him in Philadelphia where other seekers were gathering to listen to his wisdom and discover the secret to this peace.

His Holiness, the Sheikh.

The Gold Metal Test

L et me set the physical backdrop for this life outside the mainstream. By the summer of 1975, when I moved to Philadelphia from Woodstock, New York, Bawa resided at 5820 Overbook Avenue in what came to be called the Fellowship House. The Fellowship House was a massive three-story stone estate home with a gabled carriage house—the entire property surrounded by gardens. It was located in what was once an elegant arbored neighborhood of Philadelphia's financially and socially privileged.

By the 1970s, these massive gentrified homes had become loci for a most peculiar, motley mix of spiritual diversity. Adjacent to the Fellowship House was the St. Alphonso's House, home to Jesuit priests who quietly prepared lesson plans for college students at St. Joseph's University, the coed Catholic university down the road. Directly across the street, cloistered nuns silently traversed the stations of the cross on the rolling parklands belonging to the Catholic archdiocese. Down the block an orthodox Talmudic yeshiva hummed with studious young men dressed in black wool *rekels*, who would speed up and down the street with their heads together, sidelocks swaying, debating Mishnah and Gemara. And finally, up the block and cattycorner to the Fellowship House in another massive, old estate home was the Philadelphia chapter for Guru Maharaji and the Divine Light Mission.

I desperately wanted to live as close to Bawa as possible, and I wanted to move into the Fellowship House. However, not everyone who came to Philadelphia was permitted to stay in the house itself, and often they had to seek lodging elsewhere. It seemed one had to actually approach the wizard himself to get permission. So, on arrival, I approached Craig, one of the house managers, and asked him to arrange an audience with Bawa to ask permission.

"I don't know," said Craig. "I don't see much chance of it happening. You see, on any given day there are at least seventy-five people sleeping in various nooks and crannies of the house—strictly separated by gender, mind you."

At night, the boys slept on the stage or in between the rows of chairs in the meeting room. Depending on floor space, the girls slept in specially designated areas such as the second-floor alcove or in the girls' room on the third floor.

Pressured by me, Craig reluctantly approached Bawa with my request and asked if I could move into the already overcrowded house. I stood behind Craig, trying to make small—as if I could hide from this being who had already demonstrated superb mind-reading skills!

To both our surprise, Bawa replied, "Put her in the Ceylonese room."

So, that summer of 1975, my world shrank to the width of a three-foot straw mat on which I slept in the middle of the Ceylonese ladies' room—where the lights never dimmed, where the chatter never stopped, where ladies carelessly stepped on my head on their way to the loo, and where a box fan whirred incessantly on high, directed at my head despite my pleas to divert its aim.

There was magic, however, to sleeping in this Grand Central Station existence. For nightly as I lay on my mat, bone weary from working at the hospital down the street, Ceylonese ladies who had known Bawa for decades chattered among themselves in amplified voices, such that tales of the Qutb authored my dreams.

One particular night, as I drifted off to sleep with the box fan breezing through my still shower-wet hair and the lights blazing full wattage, I listened to Meera relate a most fantastical story. It seems that one afternoon she and others had gone driving through the Sri Lankan countryside with Bawa. When they stopped alongside the river to watch a herd of elephants bathing, several of the elephants broke away from their mahout, ignoring the harsh blows from his sharp metal *thotti*[3] and surrounded their car.

As I struggled to stay awake, I could hear Meera. "Aiyō!" she shouted. "So much chaos! We were screaming! The mahout was shouting, and the elephants were trumpeting!" Apparently, the elephants had encircled the car. One elephant lay next to the car, another laid his head on the windshield, while a third snaked his trunk through the window to touch Bawa. After asking the mahout to sheath his goad, Bawa stroked the beast, as tears fell from its eyes. "Yes, the world is cruel and will beat you as they have me. But go back and do your duty, for your Father knows and will deliver you from this bondage." Gracefully, the beast withdrew its trunk from within the car and rejoined the rest of the herd, who regrouped in some kind of order so that together they bowed to Bawa, trumpeted in salutation, and then returned to the river.

Some weeks later, I graduated to a spot in the girls' room on the third floor. Here, thirteen girls slept shoulder to shoulder with just enough room for our mats and then none, all our worldly possessions crammed into a three-tiered, plywood cubby above our heads. Through the thin

---

[3] *Thotti* is a sharp metal hook used in the training and handling of elephants.

floorboards, we could hear sounds from Bawa's room and the meeting room below us.

Previously, the Fellowship House had been owned by a Jewish synagogue, whose congregation had converted the first floor into a meeting room. Rows of red leather, folding cinema chairs faced a low dais of sorts, which was surrounded by a three-foot-high, spindled railing. It was from here that I heard Bawa speak for the first time, giving a powerful discourse about the nature of truth and reality.

When I entered the meeting room, Bawa was already in full force. He sat turbaned and in full lotus, ballerina erect on an emerald green chair. Words tumbled out of him in a rapid, high-pitched stream with the force of a river during a spring thaw, while his hands arced thorough the air like a conductor. I didn't know at the time that the turban was litmus to the power of delivery. A few weeks later Maureen, a long-time devotee, leaned over to me at the beginning of a discourse and clued me into the secret. "Watch out! He's wrapping his turban! Whenever he wraps his turban that way, the discourse is a humdinger!"

Sure enough, Bawa shook with the powerful download of consciousness streaming through his body. Like a human transformer, he translated this divine frequency into word, in this case Tamil, and somehow a translator miraculously tracked this brisk course of Tamil into English. He was talking about truth. He had already made the case for what truth was *not* and was building the argument for what was real and indisputable. Suddenly, he was talking about gold, saying that if one wanted to know if what he'd found were fool's gold or real gold, he had to dip the specimen in acid. If the specimen were real gold, it would come out untarnished.

He had my full attention by then. He was saying that on the spiritual path one had to dip *everything* into the acid of wisdom to verify its worth. I looked at him in disbelief. Was he telling me I had to question even him? I thought, *Do I have to put you to the acid test to question whether you're the real McCoy?* He caught my eye and nodded yes. This was curious, totally dissimilar to my experience with other worldly and spiritual leaders, who proudly held their authority above challenge.

Absorbed in this thought, I lost track of the dénouement of the discourse until I become aware of the silence. Bawa was sitting breathless in the chair, drenched in sweat like a prizefighter at the end of the tenth round. Someone brought him water, while another dried him with a towel. Then gracefully, he untangled his limbs, stood up, stepped into the crowd, and started to weave his way through the throng. As he made his way back to his room on the second floor, he stopped here and there, touching this one on the cheek, that one on the top of the head, pinching babies' cheeks, all the while grinning like a delighted innocent, who was ready to burst.

I never forgot the gold standard or qualitative metal test. With regard to Bawa, I lived alongside him at the Bawa Fellowship until his passing in

1986. For all those years, I was able to witness and question the veracity of his actions, both publicly and privately. In all those years with him, I never witnessed anything other than complete integrity and trustworthiness. And in all that time, he spoke very little of himself, always pointing toward the Creator, saying that His was the His-story we needed to study. As an aside, forgive me that I refer to His holiness in the familiar of Bawa, for Bawa translates as father and this wise man, *Qutb* of the age, messenger of wisdom, became my father in every sense of the word. With regard to the rest of my life, the gold metal test has proved invaluable for this little Pollyanna to protect herself from wolves in sheep's clothing.

I remember in the beginning, certainly not all, but many of the men who came to Bawa were longhaired, bearded hippies and the women, barefoot flower children. In their personal search for truth and understanding, many had dropped out of school and wandered the globe from country to country, sampling alternative religions, philosophies, drugs, sex, and gurus along the way and were pretty much at loose ends. Bawa rectified this fairly quickly, saying that God's children should be beautiful and that one should be able to see the light in their faces. He also explained that God speaks to man through his conscience, so, it was imperative that the speakers be kept in working order. Accordingly, static-causing drug stashes went into the toilet, and people showed up clean-shaven and coiffed pretty quickly.

Some of us global travelers complained about being situated in Philadelphia. "But Bawa," we argued, "why Philadelphia with all its sirens, gunshots, and racial tension? I mean, why not some place beautiful like Hawaii or at least the countryside or the mountains?"

He shook his head and chuckled. "So you think you can know who you are by standing on your head in a cave? No, if I put you in the jungle among all the animals and if you can find peace, then you have learned."

He also talked about the ant and how the ant is industrious and self-reliant and does miraculous duty with its limited intelligence. No one has to tell the ant to pick up his fallen comrade. Singularly, he carries his companion back to the nest. Man, on the other hand, endowed with seven levels of consciousness, struggles in the world and requires four to carry him to his grave. Spurred by this wisdom, those of us with holes in our résumés gradually went back to school or work—much to the delight of our parents, I might add.

3

Songs, Cooking Lessons, and Fairies

Bawa's persona was fabulously magnetic. The trick, however, was to keep pace with this little brown man, who was extraordinarily energetic and industrious despite his age, which rumor had was in the neighborhood of a hundred and ten or twenty. A typical day started somewhere around four in the morning. I remember one morning waking to one of Bawa's spontaneous explosions of song. "Wake up! Wake up!" he sang. "Listen to the birds. Hear how they sing in praise of their Creator. Wake like these little birds and praise your Lord!" Often he sang spontaneous songs like this, always in praise of the divine.

As dawn rolled seamlessly into day, people packed into his room. They came heavy and burdened, carrying their sorrows and worries, which they placed at his feet. They brought marriage problems, money problems, and health problems. He listened and responded compassionately and offered them the wisdom by which they might free themselves from these troubles.

I marveled the way he spoke each person's language. If they were Christian, he spoke about Jesus. To Jews, he spoke of Moses or Abraham. To Muslims, he recalled Muhammad or Ali. To Hindus, he told long, mythical tales, peopled with the likes of the four-armed Lord Vishnu and his beloved Lakshmi, mounted on the giant, golden Garuda. To scientists he spoke of atoms and particles. And for atheist, he shattered the limits of intellect, opening the possibility of faith.

Abruptly, Bawa might switch gears, calling for pots and pans, potatoes and cabbage. We would muscle thirty-gallon cooking pots up to his room and set up culinary quarters at the foot of his bed. We would chop and dice while he directed. He was very exacting and wanted all the vegetables to be cut "just so" to assure that they'd cook evenly.

Cutting Vegetables in Bawa's Room

As we chopped and peeled, he would tell us about the medicinal value of the different spices, as he was well versed in ayurvedic medicine. "Turmeric is a germicide and kills many microbes. Fenugreek seeds are good for constipation. Black pepper rids the body of excess heat and water. Radishes, both red and white, are germicides and can help clear the lungs of infection." I still have scraps of paper and little notebooks on which I had recorded these and other bits of information or pearls of wisdom from informal discourses.

Entry, October 12, 1982: Advice to Michael Green, concerning his son, Kabir, who was feverish and congested in his chest. "He's eating too many plums and peaches. These are cooling to the lungs and increase mucus production. Decrease these for now and have him eat apples instead."

The menu was varied. We made lemon pickle, garlic curry, potato curry sandwiches, spicy French Fries, and thick, sweet spiced coffee or tea. Sometimes in the winter, we would make great batches of herbal cough medicine—yummy, sticky stuff, with a kick of ginger and cayenne.

And one time, we made fairy food! I'll never forget that! Fairy food was all things sweet! Ingredients: honey, sugar, brown sugar, jaggery, maple syrup, all different kinds of fruit—apples, peaches, plums, pears, oranges, bananas, mangos, papayas. I've never tasted anything like it since.

While we made fairy food, Bawa told us about fairies. He told us how they speak Arabic and live in colonies, deep within trees, and how they can change form. He explained that fairies have a fascination with humans and love to get as close as possible to observe them, but can shape shift if they think they have been spotted.

As we sat there on the floor in his room, measuring out vast quantities of cinnamon and cardamom, he told us a story about himself and how as a child, the fairies were delighted with him and stole him to play with. He explained how they took him to a fairy colony deep inside the earth beneath the tangled roots of a tree and then returned him home safely. This sugary, ambrosial concoction that we were making was in honor of that memory.

As I listened to Bawa, I felt such a bond of comradery, as memories of my own childhood fairy offerings seeped through from the hidden depths of my unconscious.

"Please, please, please let them be gone! I hope they're gone!" I whispered to myself as I crawled into the cool, moist darkness under the leathery-leafed ligustrum in the backyard. The day before, using an erector set of grass and twigs, I had built an elaborate altar. I had fashioned a bowl of sorts with teeny-tiny coquina shells, into which I'd set my sugary offerings of Sugar Smacks. I was so intent on befriending these beings of light, who were for me reassurance of goodness.

Readjusting my glasses, which had snagged on a branch, I squinted into the darkness. *Yes! They're gone!* I sighed with relief at seeing my empty bowl. It was always such a delight to discover the altar bare. And no, I never entertained that notion that our dog, Robo, or some scavenging raccoon had eaten the enticements. Why would one ever impose reasonable thinking on fantastical adventures?

Apparently, I spent so much time out in the garden with my fantasies that when I was not to be found, my mother in exasperation would send one of my siblings looking for me, suggesting, "Try the garden first. She's probably out there, counting the stamens and the pistils." Somehow the fact that Bawa and I shared these fairy stories made me feel oddly vindicated in my fascination with fairies.

Into the Garden of Life

Into the garden of life,

Dancing on light beams and sparkles,

Come houris and fairies alike,

Authors of innocence and purity.

Scripting a moment of joy,

They weave droplets of rose scent and violet

Into the cool night air.

Chorales of laughter and bird song

Swirl softly on whispers of wind,

Enlivening heart and spirit

For each who is willing to know

That for goodness

There

Is

No

End.

His Holiness Cooking

Hunger, Disease, Old Age, and Death

It was not until years later that I understood that these cooking sessions, which were ostensibly to feed our hunger, took on more profound levels of healing. Among other things, Bawa in his wizardry was shattering the stigma of body image, which dogs American society and on a deeper level keeps the ego shackled in body identification. As Bawa kept cooking, we kept eating, and of course, some got rounder. I remember a friend of mine, whom Bawa lovingly called Moon for her dark, cool beauty. As Moon plumped with the rest of us, Bawa playfully teased her by editing her nickname from Moon to Big Moon, certainly a challenging moniker for most American females of my generation, touched by the Twiggy media movement, which outlawed Rubenesque.

This "feeding thing" was having an impact on me as well. I walked into Bawa's room one afternoon. The room was pretty full, with perhaps fifty people or so, everyone just sitting around. Bawa called to me in his high pitched voice, "Come here." Unsuspecting, I walked over to his bed, where he produced a tape measure and proceeded to take my measurements and call them off to one of the girls across the room to record. All eyes were on me, mind you. I was dying as the numerical proof of my bodily imperfections microphoned through the room to all the men and women, focused on me at Bawa's bedside. I stood there in my self-imposed shackles of humiliation, recalling a cruel, childhood ridicule, "Fatty, fatty, two by four, couldn't get through the bathroom door!"

What a set-up! No one in the audience knew what Bawa was doing, really doing that is. But I certainly did. Like some shaman, coaxing a jinni, Bawa with his tape measure called up those demonic thoughts of self-loathing, which were starving me of joy. He exposed those thoughts to the light of truth, where they began to fizzle and lose their power over me.

Shortly after this tape-measure incident, a young girl came to Bawa and explained her distaste and almost revulsion toward food, making a pitch for abstinence and fasting. Bawa listened to her tirade and then oh-so-lovingly said to her, "Oh, but my child, when you sit down to eat, you should only see love. When you look at your food, you should think, 'Oh my, look what my Father has given me. Look how much He loves me.'"

Years later, when I was looking for permanent work, a friend suggested that in between postings, I could pick up time at the Renfrew Center, a world-renowned clinic for eating disorders. I was an OB nurse, mind you, and not remotely interested in eating disorders. But in need of work, I followed the suggestion. But oh boy! Who would have thought! What a divine set-up!

At the Renfrew Center, I took care of girls who were sub-Saharan thin, some so thin that they had to be maintained on complete bed rest to conserve energy, girls who were losing their teeth, their hair, their periods from self-imposed malnutrition. It took some real honest self-inspection, but eventually, I came to see elements of myself in those girls and realized the extreme degree of mental, emotional, and physical starvation from which Bawa had healed me. Perhaps out of gratitude for my healing, it has become my secret mission to sprinkle loving words of wisdom like pixie dust along the trail for others who might similarly be starving.

On a typical day, once the cooking sessions in Bawa's room were complete, Bawa might go "rounding." He'd call for a car and driver. Everyone wanted to go on those excursions, and people would shrink themselves into ridiculously tight spaces to hitch a ride. Bawa asked to be driven into the neighborhoods of Philadelphia. He wanted to see for himself how everyone lived, the very wealthy as well as the very poor. He wanted to know the suffering of the people firsthand.

Those roundings often resulted in discourses. I remember after returning from one of these excursions, he commented about how he noticed that all the houses of worship, whether they be church, synagogue, or mosque, were vacant except for a few hours a week. As the car cruised the neighborhoods, Bawa muttered, "Locked and closed and empty. Locked and closed and empty." Obviously disturbed by this lackadaisical approach to devotion, he exclaimed that man, the noblest of God's creations, should praise God with every breath. With each of those 43,242 daily breaths, one should praise the Creator. On the exhalation, discard all qualities or thoughts of limitation or separation, and with every inhalation confirm the glory and perfection of the All.

Another time when he was rounding, the car passed a cemetery. Bawa asked all kinds of questions about burial in America. He was shocked at the cost of funerals in this country. When he got back to the fellowship house, he sang a long, mournful song. "O God, what kind of world is this today that one has to pay to be born and pay to die?" As I sat there listening, his mournful notes began to erode my youthful shield of immortality, dimming the party lights for this fiddling grasshopper. I sat there lost in thought as he explained that proper burial was essential to the journey of the soul and should be considered and upheld as an inalienable right due every individual, regardless of status.

Bawa continued to pluck this tune about death and dying, a tune, by the way, that was most irreverent to youthful ears. Soon, however, I recognized it as central to his teachings on both a spiritual and physical level. On a metaphysical level, he spoke about man's need "to die before death" to the false self. And on a physical level, he spoke about the need for proper burial practices. Insidiously, this theme wound its way into our existence, so that by 1980, in response to Bawa's guidance, our poor little fellowship had scraped together and purchased a plot of land where we could create a cemetery.

Not long after this lamentation, I was sitting in Bawa's room one night. I was tired and nodding off. As I listened in between snores, Bawa told the story of creation, explaining how the soul needed to be housed and how God requested of each of the elements a willingness to embody the soul, and how all the elements, except the earth, refused the duty. I shrugged myself, trying to stay awake. Next, he explained that man had a debt to the earth for this real estate contract and that upon his physical death, must repay the loan in full. The earth must go back to earth—that is, into the ground.

What did he say? I gave myself another shrug and straightened up. He had my attention now. So, I thought to myself, *What about cremation?* I mean really! It made so much more sense than burial. No holding all that real estate hostage to dead bodies and all.

He continued the story and was describing judgment day and how each part of the body must stand before the Creator for an accounting about the good or the bad deeds they had performed. He explained that the tongue must be witness to what it had said (ouch!). The ears must declare what they had heard (ouch!) The hands must say what they had touched (ouch!). And so on. I was ouching in my mind as I recalled all the bits of life that I thought could be mentally swept into the trash as if they never happened. I had not realized that just like on a computer, all those offenses sat there in the trash bin of my unconscious as future evidence, for only purity could permanently delete the items in my trash bin.

Bawa continued the story. Now he was talking about the moment of death. He was explaining that consciousness remained with the body until the body was interred, that the individual could not move or speak, as though anesthetized, but could feel and hear.

What! Now, I was not just mentally ouching but screaming. What? Can hear! Can feel! I was shocked and appalled as the import of this explanation began to sink in. My mind started thinking about near-death survivors, who described something similar. Suddenly, another disturbed listener squeaked, "But Bawa, what then of cremation?"

Graphically, Bawa blew all my ideation about the logic and practicality of cremation out of the water. Horrified, I listened as he described the crematory process in graphic detail and how the body essentially melted, with consciousness *feeling* each and every thermal spark and flicker. He described how as the flames worked their way up the body and reached the level of the chest, the heart would burst and the soul, in its effort to escape the body, made the corpse jolt upright, hence the practice of weighting the corpse with logs. Next, he described how as the fire reached the level of the head, the brain would burst and wisdom would depart.

I was done. Fried. (Sorry.) I could not hear any more. I had so much to think about. You see, at this time, I was in nursing school and I felt that this "capital D" thing was just dogging me. I had so many questions. What about transplants? What about artificial insemination? What about test tube babies? What if all these brilliant, scientific innovations were built on similar ignorance?

Miracles

In the early days, I witnessed many miraculous events around this unassuming, little man. These were not Bible-thumping, boisterous, evangelical, showstopper performances. Rather, they were matter-of-fact, mundane, "But of course!" understatements of grace.

I recall the time, my five-year-old son was sick with one of those mysterious and worrisome childhood ailments. I had nursed him through the night as best I could, holding his feverish little body. I watched helplessly as every few minutes it contracted rhythmically in spasms, which were not unlike labor pains and caused his little person to scream and thrash around. My pediatrician was of little help, simply offering, "Give him ginger ale and pretzels. I'll see him in the morning."

Ginger ale was not the hoped-for magic bullet. By morning in response to my son's cries of, "Take me to Bawa!" I found myself, screwed tight with exhaustion and worry, standing in front of the sheikh. I stood behind my towhead tot, as he looked up, trusting and expectant to this bearded wise man, who had managed to capture his respect and his heart by nicknaming him Superman and sneaking him Hershey's kisses. I watched as Bawa solemnly placed his hand lightly on top of my son's head and invoked the grace and mercy of God, *"Bismillāhirahmānirahīm,"*[4] and then grinned and announced, "Superman, go outside and play!"

With the ceremony concluded, my little man was delighted and all too happy to skip right out of the room. I, on the other hand, was a little stunned and could not move. This had all happened so quickly. My mind argued against the miracle just witnessed. What do you mean, Go outside and play? Mentally I cried, *No, no, no! Bawa, you don't understand! It's not that simple. He's sick! I mean really sick! I mean I've been up with him all night. You can't just make it better that easily.* Oh, those laser eyes skewered me *big time.* I felt myself shrivel under Bawa's gaze of contempt, which seemed to scream, "You doubting Thomas!" For my son, the cure was complete, and he tugged my hand, pulling me in the direction of the door. My mind continued to argue the reality of what it had just witnessed.

---

[4] *Bismillāhirahmānirahīm (A):* An invocation meaning, "In the Name of God, the Most Merciful, the Most Compassionate.

Dazed, I let innocence and faith lead me out of the room. "Come on, Mommy! Let's go play!"

His Holiness Giving Candy to the Children

Another poignant miracle-memory for me was the time my childhood friend, Pat, came to visit Bawa. It was one of those typical, early-morning sessions in which Bawa opened the doors to his room, allowing visitors transparency into the inner sanctum of his world. This was no Oz where supplicants were veiled from the wizard.

Pat and I had arrived early, to catch the worm, so to speak. I was anxious for her, anxious that among all the throngs of petitioners that she get to ask her question. *Tap, tap, tap.* Someone tested the microphones. A voice behind us asked us to scoot forward. There was a shift and rustle as latecomers squeezed into the room. As the room filled beyond normal capacity, I fretted inwardly that Pat would not be well positioned to ask her question. I need not have worried. Before I knew it, with eyes twinkling and hands to his heart, Bawa had already charmed her. "My love you, my daughter. What brings you here? Do you have any questions?" Pat explained the plight of her childless state and explained that after years of trying, she had finally scheduled an appointment at a fertility clinic in a few weeks. Then bashfully, she added that she had hoped that maybe Bawa might be able to help.

The room got silent—silence so deep that you could hear the tick, tick, tick of the vintage wall clock on the far side of the room and the clatter of cooking pots from the kitchen below. Everyone was watching Bawa, who sat in his usual double lotus posture on the bed but who had become totally absorbed and stared at his hand. His right elbow was anchored at a ninety-degree angle in his lap, with the palm up and facing him. His full focus was on his palm. Quietly, he studied his palm, nodded now and then, and occasionally mumbled something inaudible. Then just as quickly, he turned his focus to Pat and told her that he could see that there had been something foreign in her uterus, an object perhaps, which had caused the infertility. With his eyes, he motioned to one of the room girls to bring him a piece of fruit. Then he called Pat forward, placed the fruit in her hands, patted her gently on the cheek, and said, "Not to worry. Not to worry. God will help you."

The audience concluded, Pat and I skootched back from the bed a little. I could feel that she was a little undone and was trying to make sense of what had just transpired. She bent her head toward me and whispered so that only I could hear. She whispered something about how she had had an IUD once and wondered if this was the object to which Bawa was referring.

She and I never talked about this incident again. But I do know for a fact that she became pregnant before the scheduled infertility appointment and that she gave birth to three beautiful, healthy children in quick succession.

In the early days, I saw Bawa look into his palm in this manner many times when people asked him things. He told them about past lives, about karmic conditions that blocked their progress, about illnesses, and about future conditions. He explained that all knowledge was available to man and that when he looked at his hand, it was like looking at a television screen, which revealed everything.

On another occasion, I wandered into Bawa's room after things had settled down from the morning crush of petitioners. He called me over to the bedside, and with that impish grin of his, he said he was going to give me an examination. I knelt next to the bed. From somewhere he produced a little penlight.

First, he looked into both my eyes and said, "Hmmm. Quit wearing your glasses, and eat more carrots and beets." Next, he focused the light on my forehead and then on the back of my head, announcing, "The forebrain and the hind brain are not communicating with each other correctly." Finally, he asked me to open my mouth, and shining the light into my mouth, he announced, "A virus has come."

Oh my, was I in a mental stew kneeling there! I didn't know what to make of all this and hoped it mere child's play. However, the brain thing had me worried. Since my arrival here, I had heard Bawa comment on numerous occasions to visitors about the dangers of marijuana, the much-used, supposedly innocuous recreational drug. According to him, marijuana left a blue haze or cloud over the brain, causing confusion and lack of concentration. Furthermore, the residual toxins from marijuana, according to him, could take up to seven years to be excreted from the body.

Holy mackerel! I thought, *That's me all right! Torpor brain!* Yes, I had smoked my share of ganja before coming to the fellowship. And now back in nursing school, I was grudgingly having to admit that my once-photographic memory was no more and that my short-term memory was shot. For the life of me, I could not remember those exact "diastolics" and "systolics" once I stepped outside a patient's room, forcing me to record each patient's vital signs immediately.

As I knelt there in a panic, fearful of early-onset, self-induced senility, I tried to comfort myself. Now, didn't I hear Bawa say that whenever the guru touches an individual, it is not without intent—that he might be changing karma, tweaking things, so to speak? Oh, I hoped so very deeply that this was indeed true and that this impromptu exam was not inconsequential and that he was accelerating the detoxification process. I took hope in the fact that the next morning I did wake with a ferocious sore throat as predicted. And yes, based on the accuracy of this diagnosis, I did think it prudent to stop wearing my glasses.

I observed these "healings" publicly only in the early years. Apparently in response to warnings that he might come under scrutiny and be accused of practicing medicine without a license, he edited his American custom. What was natural and culturally acceptable in Sri Lanka did not float here in Rome, so the public healings stopped. Bawa seemed undaunted by this curtailing of his actions, for I recall his saying that it was Prophet Jesus who had been charged with raising faith through the performance of miracles. His mission, on the other hand, was to bring wisdom—wisdom that could free man from suffering and help him establish peace of mind. Furthermore, he made it very clear that all miracles and mind readings were mere parlor tricks and took on importance only if they furthered someone's connection with God and truth.

His Holiness as a Young Man

Social Work

Bawa didn't just talk; he taught. He demonstrated. I remember a particular incident. I walked into the room one afternoon, and there was a man kneeling at the side of Bawa's bed. Head bowed, in a soft voice, he explained that he had recently been released from prison. He had no money and no job and did not know what to do. The room quieted. Bawa's hands silently smoothed the folds of the handkerchief in his lap. After some time, he started asking questions, trying to find out what skills this gentleman might have. "Nope," he could not do this and, "Nope," he could not do that. Finally, exhausting his skills list, Bawa asked if the gentleman could drive, to which he answered, "Yes." Without missing a beat, Bawa looked out into the crowd of people surrounding his bed and said, "Money, money, money!" Quickly, bills started making their way to the front of the room.

Oh, I was so totally alert now and thought to myself, *Money is the big corruptor. You blow this, man, and I'm out of here! One stinky move, and I'm out the door.* I realized that this was one of those acid test moments. Mentally I challenged him. *Okay, Bawa. Are you gold or fool's gold?*

I watched as Bawa made piles of money on his bed and meticulously counted each bill, adjusting all the bills just so. I studied the way he touched the money. It was as though he were collecting old grocery store receipts, not Federal Reserve notes. There was a most peculiar sense of detachment, void of any charge or magnetism reflective of avarice when he touched those bills. Someone at his side carefully documented each contribution. Every now and then, a new person came into the room and walked up to the bed to make a donation. I remember Bawa scolded one woman, "Take this back. You cannot afford to give this much. There's no wisdom to giving charity that hurts yourself."

Calculations complete, Bawa called the man forward, asked him to hold out his hands. Placing the money in his hands, he said, "In God's name, I give you this money. I want you to buy a truck. You can make a good living with this truck and take care of your family. I want you to go down to the Food Distribution Center and buy vegetables. Take those vegetables to the restaurants. The restaurant owners will pay you a profit for delivering them." To his credit, this gentleman obediently did as Bawa advised and completely turned his life around. For myself, I was thrilled that Bawa had passed the acid test. Furthermore, I marveled at how this little brown man from Sri Lanka, purportedly uneducated and illiterate, had bested our prison system's efforts at rehabilitation.

His Holiness Drawing

Dead Rats, Hazing, and Illumination

There was a certain kind of hazing that happened among the girls around Bawa. If you passed muster, you became what was called a "room girl" and had certain privileges, such as being able to assist Bawa in projects or accompany him when he went rounding. As a newbie, I didn't have any friends on the inside and was a bit wary. The day before, as I was entering the room, one of the room girls greeted me with, "Boy, you'd better quit wearing that patchouli! Bawa says it comes from the sex glands of a deer. And by the way, your eyebrows need plucking." The eyebrow thing really took me for a loop because I could not see any bearing my hair follicles had on entry into the room, and as for smelling like a musky ungulate, I was pretty certain Bawa would have been less scathing in his assessment of my scent.

All in all, I was dying to sleep in Bawa's room. Being able to sleep in his room at night was like winning the lottery. Real estate being limited made the experience even more precious. Oh, I know, dear reader, I can hear you now. "What! Sleep on the floor in the guru's room! Yeah, sure! I can only imagine!" Now, let me clarify this sleeping-in-the-guru's-room thing. In this modern, upside-down, and backward, Sodom and Gomorra culture we live in, the concept of politically correct has come to distort the definition of morality such that *anything goes*. Innocence is violated so regularly and insidiously that few individuals today are capable of imagining the concept of virtue—or imagining a virtuous being, devoid of deception, perversion, disrespect, or self-business. I can tell you from experience, as can everyone who knew Bawa Muhaiyaddeen, that His Holiness was a most rare, pure individual, devoid of base human desire, and that there was never distortion or blemish to this purity in thought or word or deed. In truth, to rest in the presence of such deep and profound safety and security was immensely healing.

As the new girl on the block, I did not have a regular space and wasn't guaranteed a spot in Bawa's room. One night, I realized Barbara was away visiting family, which meant she wouldn't be sleeping in the room. So, seizing my golden opportunity, I lay down my mat. It was late, maybe one or two in the morning, and all the girls had finished lugging in their bedding. The floor had been vacuumed, the TV was off, and all the good nights had been said. No sound. I thought to myself, *Wow, I made it! I'm in!*

All of a sudden Bawa popped up and shouted, "What's that smell! Turn the lights on! Baby Mother! Everybody! There must be a dead rat! Find it!" Girls scrambled out of their sleeping bags, each one eager to be the hero who might deliver the offending trophy. They scattered around the room, opening and closing cupboards, upending trashcans. As if Bawa had said, "Off with their heads!" they scurried frantically everywhere—out into the alcove, into the hall, into his bathroom and the second-floor kitchen. Each time they came back, he sent them out again to track down the stinker.

Stinky Smell

I hid in my sleeping bag, trying for invisibility, and watched all this, totally appalled—appalled because I knew where the dead mouse was. You see, I had been having a particularly hard time digesting this new diet of spicy vegetable curries, which dominated the menu here at the fellowship, and had a horrific case of flatulence.

After about fifteen minutes, Baby Mother, who led the search, returned, admitting defeat, "Bawa we can't find it." Once again, the lights went out, the room got quiet, and I began to relax, thinking things were safe. But all of a sudden, there in the dark, Bawa started talking about farts. He went on and on. He started laughing about elephant farts and how they're the worst. Then he chuckled. "Now when Meera farts, it's worse than an elephant's fart." One by one, all the girls started snickering, and I knew he knew and I lay there mortified, just waiting for him to blow my cover. I lay there frozen in embarrassment, just expecting that like some childhood bully, he would betray me and expose me to my peers. But just as suddenly as it all started, Bawa announced, *"Nerum atch!* Times up! Go to sleep!" and the room went still. Lying there in the dark, I thought to myself, *I think I like this guy.*

In complete contrast to this awkward night of initiation was another night of unforgettable grace. It was around one in the morning. I had schlepped my bedding down from the girls' room on the third floor to Bawa's room. I sat off to the side, waiting to see if there would be room for me. Girls buzzed around the room, readying things for sleep. Once the vacuuming was complete and the lights dimmed, I noticed an open space at the foot of Bawa's bed. Quickly, I rolled out my bedding and lay down. Surrounded by the sounds of giggles and good nights, I drifted off to sleep.

At some point during the night, in some kind of altered state of conscious, I sat up on my mat and looked at Bawa, who was now sitting up on his bed. I asked him what he was doing, to which he replied that he was waiting for his guru.

Dang! I thought. *Shazam! Bawa's guru! Now that's something I'm not gonna miss! Man oh man! Bawa's guru!*

I sat there expectantly in the dark. Suddenly, the room began to pulse with the most incredible celestial light and sound. The light was brilliant, almost electrical. It glowed and pulsed, yet was cool. The sound had a shimmery, musical quality, almost crystalline. In amazement, I cried out, "He's here! He's here!" But then, I began to cry because I realized that I was in the presence of something so very profound, yet so completely unintelligible to me. And just as suddenly as the light appeared, Bawa in real life sat up on his bed and asked that the microphones be set up. He proceeded to speak for four hours, nonstop, untranslated. I sat there plugged in, listening, hoping to get a bead on what was going on. Periodically I whispered to Baby Mother, who knew a bit of Tamil, "What's he saying? What's he saying?" only to be shushed.

Later in the morning, about ten o'clock, Bawa's room opened to the general public. As the room filled, I pondered whether I should chance asking about what I had experienced the night before. You see, on occasion, people would relate to Bawa these incredible mystical experiences that they had experienced during their meditations, only to be told essentially that their imaginations were much too keen. I really needed to know whether what I had experienced was real or some figment of my imagination.

I sat there waiting for the room to quiet and for Bawa to open up the morning session for questions. My heart was hammering away in anticipation, for to ask Bawa a question was to sit on the hot seat. One never knew whether that blazing light of wisdom might come down like a sword or like a kiss. Screwing up my courage, I raised my hand and explained to the translator about last night's experience.

Bawa sat there like a stone, quiet and collected. Gently his hands smoothed and folded the cotton handkerchief in his lap into perfect squares. Then he looked up at me, into my eyes. "Child, what you saw and heard last night was real. Last night I had a vision of the destruction of the world. Because of this, I called a meeting here in this room of all the prophets, the angels, the saints, the *auliyas*[5] to discuss how to avert this devastation." He then explained that there is an organization in the unseen realms, called the Assemblies of God, comprised of various sub-committees—each committee focused on a specific need such as health,

---

[5] *Auliyas* (A) Saints; those favored by God; guides; holy ones of Islam.

education, finances, or global security. He explained that he had been asked to head this organization and that he had convened a meeting in his room to discuss matters of world peace. He explained that positioned as I was at the foot of his bed, I had "entry" to this meeting.

Staggered by what I was hearing, I managed to squeak, "But Bawa, I couldn't understand. I didn't understand that light and sound. I couldn't translate it into meaning."

Very firmly he said to me, "Erase your tapes and you will understand what you saw and what you heard."

As that morning's public session wound down, Bawa called various translators and people involved in publishing into his room and instructed that those four hours of talks be immediately translated and published. As per instructions, they were published as the two volumes titled *The Guidebooks.*

I never did get to sleep at the foot of the bed again, and I am still working to erase my tapes so I can have a have another go at that light.

King Solomon

Bawa summed up the human condition in the phrase, "Hunger, disease, old age, and death." He repeated this phrase often enough that it resonates in my memory, almost like a mantra. I began to notice hunger as a major theme intertwined in the teachings.

Sometime during the summer of 1975, Bawa was invited to speak at Leonard's house in Ventnor, New Jersey. I and about forty other followers spent the better part of the morning playing soccer on the beach and jumping the waves in the rather rough surf. I remember thinking how all-American and normal the day had seemed in contrast to all the other days I'd spent around this mysterious little brown man from Sri Lanka. Physically spent, we all crushed into Leonard's beach home, our bodies "oragamied" into ridiculous shapes to maximize listening space on the living room floor.

I sat there with my knees tucked up to my chin to listen. Bawa stories were fantastical, populated with ghosts and demons, kings and paupers, palanquins and flying carpets. On this particular day, he told the story of *King Solomon and the Fish.*

As I gradually lost feeling in my legs, I listened to this long, fanciful, ornate tale of how King Solomon had dominion over the jinns and the fairies. Being prideful of all his power and prosperity, he arrogantly boasted to God that he wanted to take on feeding all of God's creations. As I perched there in my scrunched and sweaty perch, Bawa told how God and Solomon argued, God saying it was impossible and Solomon demanding a trial.

Granted a one-day, one-meal trial to feed the creatures of the sea, Solomon summoned his servants and slaves to bring food to the water's edge. Standing proudly over his offerings, Solomon clapped his hands, whereby a huge fish leapt out of the ocean, shouting, "Feed me! I'm hungry!"

I was watching Bawa. His arms were flapping and gesticulating. He was talking fast, on a roll. Every now and then, he had to pause and let the translator catch up. The story continued as Solomon's lackey's frantically shoveled food into the fish's mouth at Solomon's command. "Feed me!

I'm hungry!" demanded the fish. This process continued until the fish had consumed all the food and threatened to swallow the jinns and fairies, as well.

Finally, in distress, Solomon appealed to God for help. And God mercifully sent down an angel to deliver sustenance to the fish. Swallowing the angelic delivery, the single drop of *rizq*[6] or grace, the fish settled and calmed, and then announced, "Ah! Now I'm satisfied." I looked at Bawa. He was the fish now, smiling contentedly, rubbing his stomach.

Next, he took up the story as Solomon, "Are you the biggest fish in the sea?" to which the fish responded, "Oh no! I am the smallest. I have seventy thousand brothers and sisters, who are seventy thousand times bigger than me." Bawa was laughing now, having fun with all this.

---

[6] *Risq* (A): Food; sustenance; the single atom of grace, coming directly from God as true nourishment.

King Solomon and Fish

Suddenly, the tempo changed as Bawa switched roles again. As God

tried to penetrate Solomon's thick shell of arrogance, Bawa's voice boomed,

"Now do you understand, Solomon! Now do you understand?" Then gently, gently as the rocky wall of Solomon's pride shattered and gave way to humility, Bawa's voice softened. "Solomon, do you see? Do you understand that all those mountains of food are like straw, like dust?"

I could not look at Bawa anymore. Somewhere during the listening, I had shattered, as memories of my own addictions haunted me. I was sitting there all snot and tears, shamelessly sobbing and hiccupping quietly to myself. As silent tears slid down my face, I thought, *He knows. He knows. He understands this canine hunger, these lustful demons, which neither coin, nor sex, nor drugs, nor food can satisfy. He understands this eternal hunger, which ravages me as well as the rest of this anorexic, obese, sex-crazed, fast-food nation. He also understands the stiff-necked arrogance that inflexibly thinks it can chart its own course.* And in that moment, I understood that, like Solomon, I must partner with that almighty power. And that like the little fish, I must learn not only to recognize, but also to receive the grace, which satisfies and which is readily available.

Politics and Patriots

While I lived in this protective bubble around Bawa, listening to discourses about peace of mind and the unity of humankind, the world went about its business of destruction. This was the 1970s. World powers bullied each other like testosterone-crazed teenagers, maniacally brandishing inter-continental ballistic weapons. Bawa was highly attentive to political events, and early mornings, after prayers, he would sit cross-legged on his bed, listening to the BBC World News on a short-wave radio. There was no funny business about these sessions. He sat alert and poised, with singular focus, almost like a stork, zeroed in on his catch. Often these sessions resulted in letters to world leaders, both religious and political. Bawa, always intent on peace, wrote powerful letters to men such as the Ayatollah Khomeini, President Jimmy Carter, Prime Minister Menachem

Begin, and President Anwar Sadat, imploring restraint, equality, and a conscience that considered other lives as its own.

One morning, during the news sessions, some of us in the room were whispering among ourselves, rolling around hippyish, "down with the establishment," socialist kinds of attitudes. Bawa's head whipped around. His eyes were fierce and penetrating like a hawk.

He barked, "What did you say?" He proceeded to scold this kind of thinking. "You should thank God seventy thousand times a day that you live in America. You have no idea, no idea what it means to live in those communist countries!" His eyes held this piercing look of knowing that quelled any romantic notions of easy equality, generated from political dogma that we might conjure.

Another morning, I was kneeling next to Bawa's bed. He was watching the news on TV. OPEC had just announced its intent to raise oil prices by 10 percent, crude oil reaching a high of thirteen dollars per barrel, a figure I might add, when adjusted for inflation far exceeds today's value. An undercurrent of mild hysteria rippled through the small crowd sitting in the room. Like Chicken Little, exclaiming that the sky is falling, we twittered, "What are we going to do? We won't have enough gas?" Worry, worry, worry! Bawa looked at us sternly. Silence. "What did you say? You should never think like that! You should never question that God can provide!" With very few words, he imparted the laser-like conviction that

God All That Is, the Creator, is all-powerful and inexhaustible and that this kind of "small" thinking or poverty consciousness was deadly. To this day, I have to caution myself from falling into the media trap of fear-based doom and gloom that seeks to limit the infinite.

Oddly, Bawa was perhaps one of the most passionately American patriotic individuals I had ever met. Whenever he was in America during an election year, he urged us all to vote. He instructed that it was prudent to include the country's leaders in our prayers, to invoke blessings of health, wisdom, and righteousness and integrity upon them. He wrote letters to the immigrant populations here in the United States, urging their allegiance and gratitude to this new country. He scolded them for draining American coffers by sending monies home to nations and families from whence they had fled, societies that had tortured, dehumanized, or failed to provide the basic needs of its citizens. He urged a sense of overwhelming gratitude for the leg up the United States offered its immigrants.

Life on the Inside—
the End to Special Relationships

As I look back and recall these nuggets of time with the guru, I begin to see a pattern whereby Bawa gradually drew me into a more subtle and intimate relationship with that thing that is the guru or wisdom. Over time there was a gradual deepening of my relationship with him, which morphed from teacher to father.

In those early, early days and weeks of my living in the house, Bawa was my teacher, and contact with him was restricted to the formal sessions when the doors to his room were open. As soon as a discourse was over and the many blessings, hugs, and handshakes complete, one of the room girls would start herding the crowds out of the room and close the doors.

Somewhat reluctantly, I allowed myself to be shuffled out of the room, walking backward so as to catch every last glimpse or morsel of this magnetic ant-man-superstar. The doors would close, and I would find myself standing there in the hallway with the strangest feeling of being abruptly unplugged.

For the longest time, I tolerated this arrangement and would wander off to the office to transcribe one of Bawa's discourses or to help in the kitchen. But after a while, it became a burning curiosity as to what went on in Bawa's room when the doors closed. Why were the room girls, many of whom I slept next to upstairs in the third-floor girls' room, allowed to stay? This curiosity grew to an obsession, where doubt and suspicion ultimately took over and created a story of supreme separation, a kind of *us and them* or *have and have* nots kind of thing. They were *in,* and I was *out.* They were privileged, and I was not. Oh, I began to burn with doubt and jealousy. I most sincerely wanted to crash this party. The bottom line was, I wanted in. But how?

Oh! But my dark mind and machinations were no match for this little brown man from Sri Lanka. No sooner had I formulated this singular, pointed desire to get in then Bawa made an announcement that if anyone wanted to come into his room, he or she had to first knock and ask permission. My mind just about went berserk with this new directive. All I could imagine was knocking on that door, sticking my head in, and having any one of those room girls chortle over the disgrace of my being denied entry. Because the idea of knocking was so absolutely unacceptable to me, I hung around the outside of the room and waited for some braver soul to come along. Like some kind of remora, I would latch on to this person or that person and hope to be passively swept in. Unfortunately, once in, I felt like an interloper and could not relax.

It never occurred to me at the time that this drama I was living was purely of my own making. The key to entry was fully in my power—all I had to do was see myself as equal, not less than or more than. Bawa was masterfully mirroring these inherited, limiting thoughts.

Well, no way José! Eve wasn't getting into paradise if she clung onto negative thoughts. If I wanted in, I had to be willing to drop all my conditioning, open my heart, and take the plunge into unconditional love.

Actually, *in* happened quite naturally once I gave up all the tortured rumination. One afternoon when the discourse ended, I just didn't get up. I sat off to the side, attempting obscurity, and oddly no one shooed me out. People shuffled out, and the door closed. Before I could really grasp the situation, Bawa lay down in meditation, and the three other girls in the room lay down on the floor next to his bed. *Holy mackerel!* I thought. *Now what do I do?* I figured I had better lie down like everyone else. I lay there, my mind screaming and my heart slamming away, fearful that any minute Bawa might pop up and say, "Would whoever's mind is screaming like that just muzzle it!"

As I lay there "angsting," a vignette from one of Bawa's stories popped into my head: A massive water buffalo was grazing by the river. A fly settled upon his horns. As the great beast foraged, his broad head moved up and down, such that the foolish fly, in its consummate arrogance, thought itself too weighty and ponderous for the beast.

Suddenly, I got the giggles. Silly me! And to think this little fly thought it could disturb the guru's mediation! Gradually, I calmed into the stillness but was abruptly startled, as one of the Ceylonese ladies exploded into the room, screeching like a parrot, *"Aiyō,[7] Bawangal[8] Aiyō!"* Apparently, there was a phone call from Sri Lanka, and the room ratcheted into high drama. And so, *in* had happened and I was hooked.

-----

[7] *Aiyō* (Tamil): Exclamatory phrase, meaning, "Oh, no!"

[8] *Bawangal* (T): Refers to His Holiness Bawa Muhaiyaddeen. In the Tamil language, respect is indicated by adding the plural suffix

The Fly and the Buffalo

Marriage

When I look back, it shocks me to see how small the orbit of my daily movements had become. Until now, the life of this tumbleweed had emerged aimlessly by the locomotion of her mind, which blew her all over the globe—from south of Capricorn to east of Greenwich. But now, she was a willing captive of a very monastic life—a life that unfolded almost totally within the four walls of the Fellowship House and the hospital down the street where she worked.

Living where I did now, inside this vortex, I listened intently to the conversations around me, trying to get the gist of what was expected of me here in this novel existence. The chatter among the women was often about men and marriage. Now girls are girls the world round and what women don't obsess about partnership? But seriously, marriage? This was the 1970s, post-Woodstock, and the hippie movement was doing some serious institution bashing—marriage taking some direct hits. What was all this marriage talk?

Apparently Bawa thought very highly about the institution of marriage. He often suggested that "marriage was half the *deen*" or spiritual path, in that the *other* offered a magnificently accurate mirror in which to see one's stray hairs. He often counseled those who fretted about the lack of a partner not to despair. "Not to worry," he offered. "There's a lid for every pot." He cautioned patience and restraint, however, discouraging the current day practice of trying on multiple lids, lest one "spoil the broth." Just a few days before, he had called all of us into his room and vociferously laid down rules of propriety. "The boys and girls in this house are like sisters and brothers to each other. The boys should be with the boys and the girls with the girls. No *kous kousing*[9] in the pantry!" I watched a young girl's face light up one morning as her boyfriend boasted to Bawa about their long-term, monogamous relationship (One year! Seriously?), only to have Bawa poke holes in his smug security by saying, "Well, you know, son, if you don't put your name on your coat, anyone who comes along can pick it up and wear it."

A few days after this monogamy-marriage talk, I was upstairs in the third-floor office. I sat there all business like, hammering away at my IBM

---

[9] *Kous Kous* (T): A slang term, meaning to gossip.

Selectric. I pretended to be focused on the discourse I was transcribing. In truth, I was trying my darndest to eavesdrop on two women who were having a good gossip. They were talking about marriage, of all things. It seemed that Bawa had a marriage list— a list of girls he wanted to get married before he went back to Ceylon. (I imagined if he were gone for long, things could get out of hand with us recovering free-spirited flower children.) At any rate, I was trying really hard to hear, so I stopped typing and faked having trouble with the transcriber. The older of the two whispered to the younger, "Now, if Bawa tells me I have to marry, the only one I'll agree to marry is Rodger."

I just about fell out of my chair. *What!* my mind screamed. *He's mine! I mean, really!* Secretly, I had already mentally laid claim to Rodger. Mentally, as all girls do (and they're lying if they tell you otherwise), I had already tried his name on for fit, and seriously, didn't Dana Hayne sound so much better than Melissa Hayne! *And besides*, my mind argued, *these other women are much too old for him!*

I had been living in the house three months now, and in that time Rodger and I had not had a single conversation outside the business of setting me up to transcribe. However, in that time, I had had plenty of time to observe him. There was a quality of carefulness and patience that I found remarkably alluring, qualities, I might add, deficient in myself. What to do? As far as I knew, I was not on the marriage list.

As I sat there eavesdropping, I was about to burst into tears at the idea of one of those women marrying Rodger instead of me. Disconcerted, I got up from my typing and fled the office. All agitated and pissy, I wandered into Bawa's room. It was early afternoon. A few girls were off to a side, doing I don't know what. Bawa was sitting cross-legged on the bed, facing the door. I sat down. Grinning, he looked at me and said, "So, who did you catch?" I looked at him dumbfounded. The girls in the room all stopped what they were doing, and all heads swiveled and looked at me.

I was so totally shocked! *Who'd I catch?* I thought. *He's got to be kidding if he thinks I'm going to say anything or expose myself in front of these backbiting women!* I didn't say anything and just sat there.

Bawa kept the pressure on. "So, who'd you catch?" He leaned forward, grinning at me, all expectant.

Oh, God, I was dying and just wanted help with all this. I was so torn and desperately wanted to cave to his prying. But not in front of all these girls, who had hazed me and kept me at arm's length.

"Where is he?" he crooned. "Where is he?"

Sheepishly I finally answered, "In my heart."

Laughing, Bawa said, "In your heart? Doesn't he have a body?"

I was just about to give in and bear my heart when Najma wandered into the room. Quickly, Bawa leaned over, winked, put finger to his lips, and shushed me. Najma proceeded to fuss over Bawa in her boisterous, familiar manner, chatting about some ongoing family matter. For about five minutes she "Ayiōed!" and "Bawangaled!" tweaking his cap straight, adjusting his *mūku toonis*,[10] and then wandered out of the room again.

As soon as she was gone, Bawa started grilling me again, until ever so softly I dared to whisper Rodger's name. Bawa chortled, slapped his thigh, and exclaimed, "He's the perfect height and the perfect age!" He saw my puzzled face and explained, "Oh, here in America, you marry these elephants to mice! I mean, look at Chris and Maureen." Mentally, I pictured them. Chris was about six eight and Maureen was, say, five one. "No worries, there though," he said, chuckling. "There are other things that make that a good match."

Oddly, the interrogation stopped as quickly as it started, and the next thing I knew, Bawa was asking for his leave, and everyone was shunted out of the room. I figured, *Oh, well. What the heck! Bawa knows now. He'll talk with Rodger and take care of everything.* So somewhat more light-hearted, I left the room.

Meera intercepted me in the hall. "Darling! I want you to come cut vegetables for me." The Ceylonese were another one of the peculiar cultural anomalies in this new existence. They seemed to command a respect and

---

[10] *Mūku tooni* (T): Handkerchief, tissue, literally "nose cloth."

privilege over and above the Americans. I was not sure how much of this was about respect for elders and the fact that the Ceylonese first discovered Bawa when he came out of the jungles, or some class thing left over from the British. At any rate, I followed Meera into the Ceylonese kitchen, where I was left with a gargantuan pile of collard greens and my thoughts. I layered and stacked the collard leaves, rolled them into tight cigars and then cut them into thin, thin, slivers. Meera dropped them into the frying pan along with the sautéed onions, chilies, mustard seeds, and curry leaves. She salted them, put a lid on, and left them to cook. When done, she sprinkled in shredded coconut. Yum! I marveled that somehow these Ceylonese ladies could make greens so much tastier than the American cooks downstairs, whose boiled and salted greens tasted like weeds when they were cooked and served.

I took my leave from Meera and on a whim stopped by Bawa's room before going upstairs. He was settling down for meditation but not *gone* yet. Lying on his side, he grinned and looked at me. "Well, did you tell him yet?" Shocked, I thought to myself, *What! What is he thinking? Me tell Rodger?* Bawa was laughing now. He said, "You two are like two lovers in a Hindi movie who pine over each other. You look out your window as you wash the dishes and when you see him, you say to yourself, 'Oh, I love you! I want to be with you! I want to hold you!' But you never talk to each other." And with that he rolled over, concluding the interaction.

I escaped to the privacy of my mat in the girls' room, where I sobbed quietly. All my dreams were shattered. I was expected to do the proposing. There was no Prince Charming to rescue me and ask me for my hand. And what if I were refused? I lay there in my self-pity until it was time for me to get ready for work.

I got dressed and headed downstairs. And as though scripted, I ran into Rodger on the second-floor landing. I screwed up my courage and started babbling, "Rodger, Bawa's been pumping me for information. He asked me to tell him who's in my heart, so I told him who's in my heart, and …"

Before I could say more, Rodger, true to his surrendered self, said, "I think we should go speak to him."

So we went to Bawa's room to place the situation at his feet. We stood bashful and innocent in front of Bawa, me in my jean skirt. We stood there waiting, not knowing what to expect. There was a lot of commotion in the room. Someone was setting up the microphones. People started streaming into the room and jockeying for a prized position at the front. Someone had brought flowers. Someone else had brought two dainty porcelain, gold-rimmed cups of tea. Suddenly Bawa started to sing. "May grace swirl around you and surround you with love and compassion and bliss." We stood there surrendered and simple, as Bawa took our hands and blessed us. With this modest ceremony, he joined our minds and hearts in a union built on faith. And so it happened. I was now Dana Hayne.

Marriage

I staggered out of Bawa's room, completely fragmented and undone. There had been no build-up to this moment, no gradual ascent to crescendo, no mulling over guest lists and seating arrangements, no dress fittings. *For God's sake!* I thought. *My wedding dress was a tea-length, faded jean skirt! Jeez. No Las Vegas hookup at the Bellagio ever happened that fast!*

Somehow there was a shock-induced memory gap between the time I left Bawa's room and arrived at work. I can still remember the moment I stepped off the elevator. I must have looked really scrambled or something because the nurses at the nurses' station got up and walked over to me. One of them shouted at me, "What's the matter with you? What happened?" When I told them I had just gotten married, they all got loud and squealy like teenage MTV groupies. Then just as suddenly they stopped and looked at me in disbelief, "So, what? What are you doing here at work! Are you insane?"

I stood there speechless. I didn't know what had just happened to me, and I certainly didn't know how to explain any of this to these very normal, very straight, church-going women. Somehow until this moment, I had been able to keep this life with the guru private and secret. Sure, the girls at work knew I was a little weird, being a vegetarian and all—but that they could handle. But ... but ... how could I explain that "Well, yeah, girls! You heard me. My guru just married me. And yeah! That's right, I don't know this man. Honeymoon? Forget the honeymoon! I'm too busy trying to figure out what the hell I'm going to tell my mom and where in God's kingdom I'm going to sleep tonight when I get home from work!"

As usual, I needn't have worried about "what's next." When I got home from work later that evening, I was met with angry glares from several of the young men in the house. Soon enough some of the girls revealed the cause for their hostility. Shortly after my leaving for work, Bawa popped up from his meditation and turned to one of the girls in the room, inquiring, "There's a room on the third floor that has a round window and looks over the front yard ... Yes? And there's several boys living in the right now. Right?"

"Yes, Bawa."

"Perfect! Tell the boys in that room to move down to the first-floor boys' room. Rodger and Dana will be moving into the third-floor room."

After this tender joining, I remember the beautiful innocence of waiting for Rodger to pick me up nightly after work. Heart pounding like some Juliet, perched on her balcony and hoping to spot her Romeo below, I'd position myself on the counter next to the centrifuge in the second-floor nursery, hoping to spot Rodger, come to fetch me, in the parking lot below. We'd walk back the few blocks to the Fellowship House, hand-in-hand, mostly in silence, for Rodger was one of few words. How beautifully healing, after being duped about my value by so many men of flattering words, to bond with someone so set on assuring me that the "inner me" was of utmost importance.

Light Beings, Palmistry, and Pharaoh

I nterspersed with all this intensity were moments of levity. I particularly enjoyed the moments right before Bawa lay down for meditation. These moments were exceptionally healing for me in their gentle tenderness. I recall one such day.

Bawa was being very light and playful. The girls gathered around and listened as he described different etheric beings, their nature, and their qualities. Of jinns he said that they were made of fire and could be impish and naughty. Next, he described angels, saying, "Now, angels are *really* tall. They have long red hair and huge wings, and they are very beautiful." Next, he described another being. He held his hand out about three and a half feet high, "About so high," he said. Those of us kneeling at the bedside were excited like little kids. "Maybe he's talking about a gnome or a leprechaun?" we suggested to Kathy, who was translating and scrambling to find some English counterpart to the Tamil names he called these various entities. He played with us like this for a few minutes, and then gently he dismissed us, lay down, and was "gone."

Another afternoon, I was kneeling by the bed. Bawa took my hand in his hands. Intently he studied my palm, looked up at me, and then gravely announced that I would be terrible with money. A little offended, I asked him how he knew that. Still holding my outstretched hand, he said, "See when you hold your hand out with the fingers together like this? See those gaps between one finger and the next? That's an indication that money will flow through your hands like water. You won't be able to hold onto it."

Suddenly, he asked me if I had anything inscribed inside my wedding ring, which I wore, as was the custom in the west, on my left hand. Proudly I boasted, "Oh, yes, I have the *Bismin*[11] inscribed inside." As he began to work the ring off my finger, he told me yet another story about the power of the *Bismin*. He told that during Moses's sojourn in Egypt, Pharaoh, hearing about the protective power of these words, had them carved above the lintel to his home. Moses in indignation railed to God, "How can this

---

[11] *Bismin* (A): Shortened form of *Bismillāhirahmānirahīm*, an invocation, meaning in the name of God, the Most Compassionate, the Most Merciful.

infidel invoke God's protection?" God then explained to Moses, "Not to worry. Yes, those words will protect him in this temporary world. But fool that he is, he is completely unaware that in the next world, he will suffer eternal punishment for his all his injustices." Carefully, Bawa took the ring off my left hand and put it on the right, explaining that the left hand represented the world and those most very precious and powerful words inscribed inside the ring must be worn on the right hand of the Father.

13

Judgment Day and Intercession

Several months later, I was sitting in Bawa's room. It was late evening and the weekend—prime time for those who worked nine-to-five. I was sitting toward the back of the room and could just barely see Bawa over the sea of heads in front of me. Bawa had just asked if there were any questions. Timidly I raised my hand and was rather startled when he locked eyes with me and indicated, "You are the one."

Oh, the moment of truth! I was still not sure who this mysterious little man was, and there was a picture forming inside me that seemed too big to be true. I really needed confirmation before I jammed the last puzzle piece into place.

The puzzle piece was a mystifying childhood memory, which for the most part lay hidden in my unconscious until something randomly activated it. Oddly enough, the memory was triggered the first day I walked into the Fellowship Meeting Room and saw the green velvet chair on the stage from where Bawa publicly discoursed.

Seeing the chair, I was transported back in time to 1953. In the flashback, my three-year-old physical self was sitting on her bed, absorbed in a most paralyzing experience. She was watching her judgment day. She stood in front of a man who was seated in a green chair. Around him, as far as the eye could see, were multitudes of souls, past, present, and future, who stood as witness to her judgment. As she stood there, she felt naked, like glass, as though he and all these millions of eyes could see it *all*. She stood there, and on some kind of holographic picture screen, the reels of her life played for all to watch. She stood there watching, horrified and humbled because now she knew better, now she knew right from wrong. But alas! Now she was totally impotent, unable to edit the reels of her life. In that moment, she understood that there need not be any other hell. This knowing and impotence to change the reels were hell and punishment enough.

I finished telling Bawa this experience. The room had gotten very quiet, and mercifully people in the room looked anywhere but at me. Bawa talked to me softly and very gently dropped the final puzzle piece into place. "Child, I was with you then, as I am now." Hot, salty tears slid down my face. Someone stuffed a wad of tissues into my hand. For me, these words were precious like a positive DNA test, confirming that I had found my father. I sat there, tears streaming down my face and thought to myself that all these years, this gracious being had watched me, watched me hang myself in knots of ignorant, karmic choices, allowing me my free will. Like the fisherman who waits patiently for his catch to exhaust itself, he waited to reel me in until my arrogance was willing to admit defeat, admit that I truly did not have the wisdom to manage my own life with dignity.

And as though that puzzle piece was not enough, Bawa dropped another. "I was watching your life, and you were headed for destruction. I begged God to save you, so He married you to Rodger." Here I really lost it and began sobbing helplessly. His chess piece played, Bawa indicated to people in the room to keep tissues coming my way and then moved on to other questioners. Through my tears, I tried to make sense of all this. *So many puzzle pieces at once!* I thought. Oh, how many times had I wondered how a girl like me, from a complicated background like mine, had ever managed to marry such a husband—a husband who would never, never, never hurt her; a man with such restraint and love for goodness that he would tolerate her moods and instability, playfully calling her Miss Up-Down, and who, unlike so many men in the world, would never, never demand that she be the source of his pleasure against her will. Miraculously, Bawa Muhaiyaddeen, this divine, merciful, compassionate being, bit by bit, was giving me back my dignity and my purity.

Loving Blessings from His Holiness

Newborns and
Separation Anxiety

I n August of 1976, Bawa returned to Sri Lanka at the behest of his long-time Ceylonese followers, who had sent hundreds upon hundreds of letters and telegrams, pleading for him to return. There was much crying and chest beating on our end, of course. "But certainly," Bawa reasoned with us, "you must understand the needs of these Ceylonese children as well." So reluctantly, we saw him off. Some of us like toddlers, experiencing first-time separation anxiety, crushed around him at the airport on his departure, scrambling for one last hug. Bawa, ever so patiently, bright and mirthful as always, assured us that distance was of no matter, that all we need do was post our letters of request in the mailbox of our hearts and that he would most certainly receive them and answer them individually.

Over the next two years, I wrote many such remote letters such that if we'd had e-mail back then, my mailbox would consistently have displayed the "not enough free data space" alert.

At the time of Bawa's departure, Rodger and I were anxiously awaiting the arrival of our firstborn, due the following spring at the end of March or early April. I was working down the street as a nurse's aide at Booth Maternity, a midwifery hospital and home for unwed mothers. You'd think this maternal atmosphere would add brilliantly to my composure as an expectant mother. However, on Groundhog Day, weeks before my due date, equanimity ratcheted into terror in less than thirty seconds when I felt a gush and spurt of warm water sliding down my legs while I stood at the kitchen sink washing dinner dishes. As the reality of the situation dawned on me, I thought, *I should've guessed the tea leaves weren't in my favor this morning when the groundhog didn't have the decency to show.*

At any rate, I stood at the kitchen sink leaking and shrieking. "My water just broke! My water just broke!"

To which Rodger, who just happened to be walking up the stairs from work, calmly responded, "So??"

"So? So? What do you mean, so?" I wailed!

Inwardly, I was thinking, *Gosh! I just wanna punch this guy's lights out sometimes! Seriously, can he really be this calm or is he really just clueless!*

Outwardly, I was wailing, "It's too soon! Too soon! The baby's not ready yet! Besides, I'm not ready! I don't have *anything!* Not a diaper pail! Not even a friggin' diaper!" So Rodger calmly bundled me and my hysteria into my coat, and off we went to the hospital to await the arrival.

At the hospital, the midwives were not too happy to see me. First and foremost, my early labor presented my friends and coworkers with additional risk. A six- to eight-week premature infant did indeed push the limits of standards of care required by our level-one, low-risk birth center. Second, I had successfully, up to this point, evaded all suggestions to attend prenatal classes and was thus, in their opinion, less than prepared for the forthcoming event. Somehow, I just didn't know how to politely convey to these women, whom I worked with, that the "Hout! Hout!" Lamaze breathing, which they held in such high esteem, was just not my thing. How could I explain to them that my "adoptive," primal father had instructed me in a breathing practice so simple, yet so esoteric, that according to him, if performed correctly, it had the ability to cure all the myriad of physical and mental diseases, complete all karmas, and establish a state of bliss and perfection, essentially rendering rebirth unnecessary? So as it was, Rodger sat next to me in the labor room into the wee hours of the morning. He sat there still and silent as the Redwoods. Resolute in his trust in God, he helped breathe me out my body, beyond the pain, until our little fellow arrived, howling and squirmy—all four pounds, thirteen ounces.

I had heard so many, many birthing war stories, where women, trying to expunge their post-traumatic demons, recounted beat for beat the hardships they endured during birth. But never had anyone explained this most exquisite, powerful, transformative moment where one's identity changed so abruptly and indisputably. With that one, final push, as this child slipped out of me and they placed him, wet and squirmy, in my arms, I was no longer *girl*. I was *mother*. And *mother* is so much more than *girl*. And this mother was so absolutely unprepared for the shock of separation when they took this new but premature, hard-earned gift from the tender nest of her breast and placed him under glass, where touch happened only at appointed hours, through tiny, glass portals.

After ten days too many of incubators, heel sticks, and bilirubin tests, the medical powers that be announced that our prize preemie was safe to take home. So, we swaddled our tiny treasure in borrowed hospital receiving blankets and carried him home to our room at the Fellowship House. He spent the next six months in a laundry basket, which Rodger had cleverly outfitted with a foam mattress and its own miniature sheets. In retrospect, I see how wonderfully unburdened we were by all the accouterments made essential in today's Babies-R-Us world of newborns— such as Boppy pillows or Snugabunny cradle swings.

Of course, we wired Bawa immediately about our son's arrival, asking for a name. During the wait, I received a "blessing packet" from my new age sister in Woodstock. Inside was what I recognized as a horoscope, but this was not my area of expertise, so all the glyphs and ciphers were meaningless. At the bottom, there was a notation: "Watch out! You have a powerhouse on your hands. This is one mighty little child." *Yeah, sure,* I thought. *What does she know?* I put the chart aside and forgot about it, waiting for Bawa's reply. Finally, several days after he was born, we received a telegram.

Western Union Telegram

Jaffna 02/09/77

Baby's Name Azeez

Pronounced Ah-Sees

From Allah's Ninety-Nine Beautiful Names

Bawa

Rodger and I looked at each other dumb, silent. Azeez? Not Michael or David. Not Samuel or even Solomon, but Azeez, a name not even remotely familiar to Western ears or cultural sensitivities! I grabbed my Arabic dictionary and hurriedly thumbed through the alphabet, *alif, baa, taa, tha, ein.* Here it is! *Azeez*— "to be mighty, powerful, honorable, precious or cherished, the might and power of God." *Go figure!* I thought, recalling my sister's horoscope. This was a name written in the stars. How incredibly perfect! *But! But! But!* I thought. *How in God's name am I ever going to tell my south-of-the-Mason-Dixon mother?*

I didn't know why I even bothered worrying. I called my mom long distance with news of her firstborn grandchild, hoping, just hoping that she would be so all consumed, busting with pride and joy that names wouldn't be of consequence. But as soon as she started ranting about how he was equally "a product of her loins as well as mine"—No lie! Her words verbatim! — and that she was just going to tell the rest of the family to call him Rosebud, I quietly, without a word of defense or explanation, set the telephone receiver into the cradle. I didn't realize at the time that I had just completely and finally severed the cord of attachments that bound and sublimated me to this prideful, powerful woman. Oh, what a master was this Bawa Muhaiyaddeen.

15

The Flower and the Tree

I n response to our pleas, Bawa agreed to return to the US and was scheduled to arrive in July of 1978. His return necessitated a lot of shuffling in living quarters, as many of the couples were living in rooms that would house the Ceylonese translators and their families when they arrived in Philadelphia. I must say that I was frantic about the thought of having to leave this strange place, which oddly had become my home, so I was ecstatic when we were given permission to move into two rooms in the three-roomed carriage house behind the Fellowship House. Yahoo! At last! A home and a room for our son! After seventeen months, I was so done with living cheek by jowl in one room!

Rodger and I launched head-on into renovating the neglected and timeworn carriage house. We spent all our free time and all our meager lifesavings to expunge the rot and peel of decades. Like some *Better Homes and Garden* bride, fueled by the maternal instinct to create a home, I merrily scraped and spackled. And like a little child, cheerfully playing with her dollhouse, I supervised the placement of all the new appliances. Let's see. The washer and dryer, matching, of course, go here. The fridge goes here. And let's see, the stove'll go here. But as the carpet layers were knee-jamming the final section of wall–to-wall carpet into place, all my dreams and romantic notions came to a screeching halt. A brief but sobering telegram arrived from Sri Lanka. It advised that a single woman, who was returning to America, would need to stay in one of our rooms, temporarily, of course, until she could find herself a suitable place to live.

Oh, I did *not*, did *not,* did *not* like this! And I made my discontent very much known, throwing a massive hissy fit, launching fireballs of outrage indiscriminately—most of them landing on Rodger. Ever ready to surrender to the guru, Rodger bundled me into our old Dodge Dart and headed down to Foam Land, where we bought a four-inch-thick piece of foam, which we nestled into the little alcove beneath the gabled window in our room as a temporary bed for our toddler.

Little did I know that I would watch my son's tiny body expand and stretch from toddler pudgy-round to gangly-long and lean over the next eight years on this precious piece of real estate as one visitor after another took "temporary" refuge in what I thought was to be my child's room. Nor did I know that for the next two decades I would coexist with a roulette of multiple families and individuals in this aerie above the print shop, where the presses rumbled like a freight train, spewing their inky fumes beneath our bed. And I certainly did not foresee that during those years, as the Israelis and Palestinians shoved each other back and forth along the Gaza Strip, arguing over kilometers, I would fight my own border wars in the shared quarters of the carriage house, absurdly arguing over centimeters.

Ah, the big question, you wonder! Why stay? Why, pray tell, did you stay? Oh, that's so simple. Love. Love, of course. Bawa Muhaiyaddeen radiated a love that exceeded the light of universes. It was a love that, when it fell upon you, outshone and dispelled all the inherited, crippling darkness of separation. To be anointed with that look of love defied description! And as if the *darshan* of this loving gaze were not enough, Bawa tirelessly offered instruction on how to merge with that love, how to find it within one's own being, how to hook it up with the thread that courses through all beings, and how to join the resonant symphony thrumming throughout all universes, all time, and all dimensions. After the first taste, I wanted more, and I wanted to learn how to cultivate this fruit myself.

It's in the looking back that I begin to see for myself how the love affair began between me and the guru. I recall a specific bookmark in the story shortly after Bawa's return. Throughout the day, I zipped through my chores and house duties—as if I could hurry the hands of time and hurry a mother's moment of freedom when her child sleeps. By night, as I read to my son, I rubbed his back and watched impatiently for his eyelids to droop. *Come on, come on,* my mind urged! *Go to sleep, little one. Just go to sleep.* As soon as I was sure of the snooze effect, I gently removed my hand from his back, quietly slipped out of the room, and made a beeline for Bawa's room.

I intended to sneak in as a casual observer but was caught off guard when Bawa addressed me as soon as I entered the room.

"*Marplay engay*? Where's your husband?" he asked.

"He's at home with our son," I answered. "Rodger said he got to spend time with you in Ceylon and now it's my turn."

"That's right," he said, nodding. But then he added, "Child, if the flower doesn't become attached to the tree, then the fragrance of the flower won't come."

I looked at him completely puzzled and thought, *Bawa, what are you telling me? Are you telling me I have to become attached to you?* I was so puzzled. All these months and weeks I had been transcribing discourse after discourse, which talked about non-attachment as the means to freedom, and here he was telling me I had to become attached to him.

And so, I entered a new era, where gradually teacher became father. My Father. And oh, there was the rub! Attached I became, indeed. And this master took me through all the permutations of worldly love, jealous love, selfish love—concepts all based on the misconception that God/love is a limited commodity.

Dana and Bawa

Silent Night

I made an absolute pest of myself after this flower and tree talk. Every night after the snooze effect set in, I beelined to the bedside. Somewhere after ten, all the petitioners, exhausted from their petitioning, drifted off to their homes, and Bawa's room emptied and quieted to the relatively few individuals of the late-night shift. As soon as the room was vacated, Bawa would announce, "bioscope," and the television went on. Like toddlers plopped in front of a show, we'd sit there mesmerized, which I'm sure gave Bawa relief from our endless needs and demands. Christine, God bless her, became my champion and snuggled me in next to her at the bedside from where she translated for Bawa whatever bioscope we were watching. Each time I'd start to make my exit, thinking, *Oh, my God, look how late it is!* she'd grab my hand, yank me back down and say, "Where are you going?"

I had no idea how emotionally crippled and fearful I was. Like some stray dog, wary from all life's beatings and rejections, I'd sit there looking straight ahead at the TV, my heart pounding and me ready to bolt. Every now and then, Bawa would reach down stealthily and pinch my cheek. I'd whip my head around in surprise. Bawa would grin and point at Christine as though to say, "She did it." Or later yet, I'd feel this tap, tap, tap on my shoulder. I'd look up to see Bawa, finger to his lips, warning, "Quiet!" and then look down to find a Pringle in my lap, which he had snuck for me from the snack tray Auntie Noor had prepared and intended for him.

I could never figure why she continued to bring him those snacks because I never saw him eat them. One by one, those chips and nuts made their way into our mouths. I'd heard about saints, breathairians, who didn't eat, who fed off of light. I had also heard that when Bawa came out of his decades-long sojourn in the jungle he complained to some of his disciples, "I haven't eaten for years! Why do you people insist on feeding me?" At any rate, I was certainly skeptical of the possibility of light feeders. But I can assure you, as the day is long, that over a period of eleven years I never saw Bawa eat a meal. The closest I ever saw to what someone might call "eating" was when he cooked for us. I'd see him take the tiniest of tastes—tiny, tiny, tiny—just enough to check the balance of salt and spices. He did drink warm water regularly, however, and sometimes a cup of barley water. Other than that, his sustenance was something far more subtle and ineffable.

When I started nursing school, my life became hectic, and there was little time to spend in Bawa's room between mothering, working, and schooling. I eagerly awaited the six-week semester break when I could spend uninterrupted time with him. This was my time with my father. Each night, I'd settle my son off to sleep and head over to Bawa's room. I'd listen to the public discourse, scrunched up in my perch behind the bed. Then as soon as the room emptied, I'd swap sides of the bed and take up residence next to Christine during the bioscope. Somewhere around midnight, the room got vacuumed and the girls lay down their mats. Unable to stay wake, they one by one fell off to sleep, leaving me alone and awake with Bawa.

I'd sit there on the floor next to his bed in the dark room, lit only by the distant flicker of the TV. For long hours, Bawa sat there with me in companionable silence as the girls snoozed around us. He sat there positioned above me in his double lotus as though on a throne of contentment, in an egoless state of still silence. How could silence speak such volumes, I wondered? Occasionally, he might reach down and stroke my hand or my cheek, but for the most part we just sat there in silence, until wordlessly he'd indicate, "bioscope off," and he'd lie down and slip silently into another dimension.

The sacred holiness of that silence was so deeply and profoundly healing. I'd hold silent vigil at the bedside until daybreak and then make my way home to greet the morning with my early riser son. Such were my holy nights. I didn't realize that this growing trust would pave the way for corrections.

Listening

Listening beyond the winds of worry,

Beyond despair's frantic screams for help,

I strain in the dark of night to hear the *Guiding Voice.*

Beyond all dissonance and discord,

Wisdom whispers, oh so softly,

"Be still and follow *Me.*

This way.

This way.

Now this way.

Follow

Me.

Follow deep within your heart.

Feel *Me* in the peace.

Settle in the sanctuary of the stillness.

Herein

Lies

The

Truth."

17

Never Be a Broker, and the Nature of the Beast

One morning not long after this, I was sitting in the alcove outside Bawa's room, waiting for the room to open. I was by myself, minding my own business, just waiting. A young woman my age, whom I kinda-sorta knew, settled next to me for the waiting. Pretty quickly, she started telling me her marital woes, which happened to shock the pants off me. Mentally, I was OMG-ing. I told her, "Why are you telling me this? I can't do anything to help you. You need to talk with Bawa. This is way too big for me."

Fortunately, the door to Bawa's room opened, and we went in. Off to the side, I made squeaky noises about this girl's situation to one of the room girls, who brought it to Bawa's attention. Before I knew it, everyone except the girl in question and a translator were swept out of the room, and I was back in the alcove waiting. The difference now was that my mind was mulling over all the nasty details this girl had downloaded to me, and I was mentally becoming vigilante to her cause.

After a bit, the room opened. I went in, and again, everyone but a translator and this time, me was shooed out of the room. The door locked, and it was just me and Bawa and a translator.

Okay! I thought. *This is scary! What is going on?*

I didn't have to wait long. All of a sudden Bawa was addressing me—*forcefully!*

"Don't you *ever* be a broker for another person!" he shouted.

Omg! Omg! Omg! I was puzzled and really scared. Broker? What was he talking about? What'd I do? My mind squirmed, negotiating innocence, for I really didn't understand the charges against me. I was so busy mentally defending my innocence that even though I was aware that Bawa was shouting, his words seemed far-off, muffled, and distorted. I was lost in some inner power struggle. My face was flushed, and I could feel my body burn with the heat of pride and self-righteousness at being, what I considered, falsely accused. *I! I! I! But! But! But!* my mind wagered.

Once again, Bawa shouted, "Don't you *ever* be a broker for another person!" Suddenly, the bubble of my pride burst, and all the bluster and resistance fragmented, and some small piece of trust and humility floated to the surface victorious, so that I was now present and receptive.

Seeing that I was finally ready to listen, Bawa softened. "Child, I'm going to tell you what's really going on in that household, and I don't want you ever to mention details of this outside this room! Do you hear!"

He then proceeded to tell me a very different story, providing facts and perspectives totally lacking from the version I had heard, which put a whole different spin on things. As he talked, my mind gasped at the totally different reality of the situation. He repeated all the facts and all the warnings several times, exhorting me to take heed. And then, once again, I found myself back out in the alcove. I sat there stunned, needing to make sense of what had just happened.

Through some divine benevolence, to this day, I cannot remember a single detail of the situation that Bawa disclosed to me. The wisdom, however, will remain etched in stone. This father-friend of mine knew that my work in the healthcare field would draw me intimately into people's private lives. He could see that this budding Florence Nightingale was green and that her haste and humanitarian verve might plunge her deep into entanglements of human suffering if wisdom did not guide each step, cautioning her to "hurry slowly" and advising her to gather more information before making the plunge to committed action.

A few days later, during a public question-and-answer session, this theme of limited perception broadened and expanded. Bawa recounted an ancient Hindu parable about four blind wise men, who encountered an elephant. Each in his limiting blindness went at the beast. One grabbed hold the tail, one the trunk, one the leg, and another the ear. They experienced the cold, ceramic smoothness of its tusk; the hard, broom-like bristles of its tail; the stout, tree-like girth of its legs; and the rubbery, flexible, fan-like quality of its ear. They knew this creature—the realness of it made all the more vital to them through their senses. Each knew so indisputably what he had experienced. Ultimately, when they convened to verify their findings, the ardent pride and certitude of each one's experience catapulted him into battle to defend his perception and his understanding of the beast. And so, an argument ensued— so rapid and atomic that none could even begin to consider the possibility that perhaps—just perhaps— there was much one did *not* know. Nor could one consider that one might have mistaken the part for the whole. As I sat there listening, I saw myself, the self-appointed authority, so like these supposed wise men, all too quick to wrestle to the ground my spouse or some other unsuspecting individual in the certainty of my knowledge.

Exhausted after years of arrogant rutting and butting, I've had to crawl off into a corner to lick my wounds. I don't like it alone in my corner. I really am a pack animal and prefer community. But how to be in community when each is so passionately defending his own perspective? How is there any hope for world peace? And then one day, alone and lonely in my corner of separation, I finally got the most basic universal law, which is that oneness, *Tauheed*,[12] all that is, whatever you want to call that thing, is unequivocally the sum of all its parts. It is mathematical law. Not fifteen-sixteenths. Not eight-ninths. Not ninety-nine one-hundredths. *Almost* doesn't cut it. Truth and unity—and by extension world peace—can only be achieved when all perceptions are considered and honored. Wisdom and humility must muzzle arrogance and foster consideration of the other, for indeed, it is law. One is equal to the sum of its parts.

---

[12] *Tauheed* (A) The indivisible oneness of God, monotheism.

Appellations

Pretty quickly, I observed that names were very important to Bawa. Those names spanned meaning from the mundane to the sublime. But always, always, always those names were loaded with meaning, like personal and private code words for each individual. When several individuals had the same first name, they each received a nickname appropriate to some personal characteristic. The Garys became Banana Man, who adored and devoured the many varieties of Ceylon bananas, and Cookie Man, who, yes, loved cookies. There was Sheena Michael, who was the youngest of the many Michael's (*sheena* meaning "small" or "little" in Tamil) and Radio *Tambi*[13] who worked for a radio station in Boston. Then there was Kitchen Princess, a South African fellow, who commanded the

---

[13] *Tambi* (Tl): Term of endearment, meaning "little brother."

communal kitchen with a stately, "just so" manner and Printing Tambi, a young Canadian fellow, who operated the ancient printing presses on which Bawa's books were printed. But my favorite moniker of all was Mango Bob, given to the chubby-cheeked daughter, born to one of the Bobs.

And then there were the exalted names—traditional Islamic names— drawn from one of the Ninety-Nine Sacred Attributes of the Divine.[14] There were names such as *Malik*—that regal, stately, most just, and equitable ruler or king; *Raheem*—the limitless compassion and mercy of God; *Saburah*— that undisturbed, willing, steady patience of God; or *Halimah*—that most-gentle, modest, unassuming, lighthearted forbearance of God.

All I knew is that I wanted a name. To have a name was to be recognized, to be part of the club. Secretly, I lusted for one of those exalted names—one of the ninety-nine. I'd sit there in the clutch gathered around Bawa, waiting, just hoping that he'd take notice and free me from the realm of invisibility by giving me a name.

And then one day it happened. Very fast, mind you. The naming "ceremony" was solemn and swift. Beaming, Bawa singled me out, called

---

[14] *Asmā'ul Husnā* (A): Literally, the beautiful names. Believed to be formless, God can only be known through the emanation of His qualities or attributes of which there are said to be ninety-nine. These names are often given to individuals to inspire noble character.

me over to his bed, leaned over and said, "A name has come. Ma'rufah. Now, *Ma'rufah* means the eternal wisdom of God." Then quickly, I was kind of squeezed, not shoved exactly, away from the bedside into the crowd as someone else negotiated the front and center position in front of Bawa.

And then my mind started. Faceless in the crowd again, I was possessed with wanting to understand this name. I got up and went in search of Sayid, a native Syrian scholar and Muslim, who had been teaching some of us rudimentary Arabic. From him, I understand that the name came from the verb *'arafa*, to know; that Mount Arafat, that sacred and hallowed site where the Prophet Muhammad gave his last and farewell sermon to his followers, also came from this same root; and that *Marifat*, a metaphysical Islamic term, which refers to the fourth stage of spiritual ascendance in which an individual merges with God, also came from this root. Now, any normal individual with an ounce of appreciation and humility would have fallen down blabbering with gratitude at the gift of such a name. But not this puppy!

This petty, audacious mind of mine was full of guff and grumble. But, but, but, it complained. It's not one of the sacred ninety-nine names. I didn't mention any of this angst to anyone but just sat there, day after day, moderately discomfited as others received one of the hallowed names.

Oh, but that clever, clever, masterful teacher, unbeknownst to me, had gotten a bead on my mind and was poised to pull the rug out from under this infectious disease of "specialness," which threatened to keep me locked in separation. A few weeks after the original naming, Bawa called me over to his bed. "A new name has come!" he announced. He leaned over, face in my face, eyes a twinkle, and said, "Bajeerah! Now, Bajeerah! That's like *all* of God's names, all of God's qualities."

Ouch! I thought. No one else in the room knew how he was playing with my mind. This was between him and me. Here I was, lusting for one, just one, of those names, and he dubbed me with one that supposedly embraced all of God's qualities.

No one, and certainly not me, knew that he was ratcheting up my mind. I and everyone else in the room assumed that he was referring to the name *Baseerah* (one of the ninety-nine), the perceptive or all-seeing one. But he had pronounced the crucial consonant *saad* as a *jeem*, altogether changing the meaning. So yes, once again, dear reader, my mind fragmented in doubt. Is it *Baseerah*, which is one of the ninety-nine (and not all of them, mind you)? Or is it *Bajeerah*, a name in the dictionary with the sole definition of "obese or corpulent." Yikes! And now what? Am I *Ma'rufah* or *Baseerah* or *Bajeerah*? Who am I, my mind shrieked! And oh, dear reader, unfortunately that was not the end.

A few months later when Rodger and I were in Ceylon, Bawa decided to stir the pot once more. It was probably one in the morning. The crushing, sweaty heat had backed off a bit. It was very still and quiet. But I was not fooled. I knew as soon as we turned the lights off, the flying cockroaches would start their aerial attacks. I'd been startled awake too many nights by one of those dive-bombing little kamikazes, crashing into my face with its hard, crusty carapace.

Some of the girls had laid down their thin, straw mats and were already stretched out on the mercifully cool cement floor, hoping to catch whatever sleep they could before Bawa popped up at three or so, like some pre-dawn warbler, singing songs of the divine. (I mean, really, how can you find fault with someone who wakes up enraptured, "choralling" in ecstasy?) I was sitting with a few girls, positioned on the floor around Bawa's bed, waiting to see if there was any last morsel to be had before Bawa announced, "Lights out." I was absorbed, watching the spare expenditure of his movements as he gracefully collapsed his legs like the blades of a pocketknife so that his feet slide out of their slippers, and he was able to pivot his legs up onto the bed in one smooth movement.

I was startled out of my concentration and realized that he was talking to me. "A new name has come. *Ma'bubah. Ma'bubah* is that quality which embraces everyone with love. And child, do understand that the name does *not* presuppose the nature of the person. One has to earn the name. Lights out! *Nerum Ach* (Time's Up)."

As usual, he had timed his delivery impeccably so as to discourage discussion. Surprisingly, I was rather pleased with this name, briefly that was, until the next morning when one of the more corpulent, well-endowed ladies cupped her hefty breasts and squealed, "Oh, no! He tried to give me that name one time, but I said, 'No way!'" Well, that just ruined it for me! I'd never made the sound association between *Ma'bubah* and boobs. *Who am I?* my mind wondered.

I stewed in my thoughts like this until the morning Rodger and I were due to depart Ceylon and fly back to the States. Our bags were packed, and I was anxiously waiting our departure. (Why is it those transatlantic flights are always scheduled to depart at the most ungodly time in the wee hours of the morning?) Time to kill. To think. Like some Sears Washer Deluxe stuck on spin, my mind agitated, who am I, who am I, who am I?

Bawa opened up the room to questions, and I mustered up the courage, or perhaps in this case, foolishness to ask my question. "Bawa, what's the significance of the names the guru gives a disciple?"

I was not ready for Bawa's reply. Until now, he'd been very patient. Like a standup comedian, who knew timing was everything, he waited until the room was really quiet and expectant. He turned to me and said, "Well, you know, you can call a dog by many names, but it's still a dog," and then looked away. End of subject. Snickers, snorts, and laughter punctuated the room. I felt my cheeks burn and wished I could just hide. I was so enraged by what I perceived as public humiliation that I could not begin to see my own foolishness in all this.

I left Sri Lanka that night for home. There were no emotional good-byes and shedding of tears. I was pissed. Done. I wanted no more of this little brown man and his head games. I was outta there. Done! Mentally, I tried to divorce and distance myself. I told no one about this but secretly held onto my anger and pride until it coalesced in my heart like a stone. I buried it beneath the drudgery and doing of everyday life and essentially forgot about it.

SIDS Babies—
Ambassadors of Faith

Some months later after my return from Ceylon, one of the Fellowship women related a most remarkably tragic and poignant experience to me. Through sobs and silences, I came to understand that a six-month-old infant, newly in her care, died while napping in her day care center. "I sent my daughter, Maya, to wake the baby from his nap because it was time for his next feeding. But when she lifted him out of his crib, he wasn't breathing!"

In detail, she described the shock and horror of finding the limp and lifeless child, the terror of calling the police, and the unimaginable remorse of having to call the child's parents. The medical examiner declared the death SIDS related, exonerating her of any wrongdoing. Nonetheless, she described the state of deep, drowning despair into which she plunged. Unable to understand this seemingly random, meaningless, and most awful event for herself, she found it difficult to reach out personally to the child's mother, whose despair she could not even begin to imagine.

She called the ashram in Sri Lanka, hoping for some scrap of wisdom or comfort from Bawa. From across oceans and continents, leagues and leagues away, Bawa caught her in her downward, drowning spiral and shouldered her to the surface. With command and knowing, he explained that there was no reason for sadness, that all was well and indeed, not meaningless.

He explained that these SIDS deaths, as we call them, were indeed not tragedies and that science would never be able to discover the real cause for their occurrence. He explained that these infants were messengers, pure souls, sent only most briefly to deliver missives from the divine. He explained that this child, likewise a pure soul, had come here to this world only very briefly with the express purpose of teaching the parents a most intimate and crucial life lesson, perhaps even a key to their own salvation. "Go now," he instructed. "Go to the mother, comfort her, and explain this truth."

As I listened, I waited for my friend to collect herself. In between gasps and hiccups, she continued her story. "I was standing at the front door, waffling, hesitant to knock when the door opened and the mother pulled me inside. 'I have to tell you something,' she said. 'Last night I had a dream. My baby girl came to me. She told me not to be sad. She told me that she was sent to give me a message and that then she had to go back. She told me many, many things. She made me promise to tell you this. She said you'd understand.'" At this point, my tortured friend broke down most totally and completely.

Ironically, some months later, a similar incident insinuated itself into my own experience at Children's Hospital, where I worked in the intensive care unit. It was the wee hours of the night. I had been assigned to retrieve the body of an infant from the morgue, as out-of-town grandparents had arrived and wanted to view the child. From the hushed whispers of the nurses, I gathered that the infant's demise was considered a SIDS death. The elevator doors closed behind me, mercifully blocking out the maniacal screams and wails of parents and family members of this infant, who had died at home and arrived earlier that day on our unit—DOA,[15] as we so impersonally called it.

Alone, I descended into the cold, sterile belly of the hospital on this most unpleasant mission. It was nighttime, and the hospital was like a ghost town. The echo of my hurried footsteps on the cold ceramic tiles

---

[15] DOA: Medical acronym, meaning dead on arrival.

spooked me as I rushed through the empty hallways, mentally fleeing the imagined angel of death.

The screaming and wailing up on the unit had almost undone me, and I was so close to losing it myself. I passed the pathology lab where there was a light on. I watched horrified as a pathologist, performing an autopsy, scooped the heart out of the prone and lifeless body of a child I recognized from our unit.

Something shattered inside me, and I ran through the empty hallways, sobbing. I felt so unsupported and orphaned, without a lifeline, and all the bottled-up stress of life —marriage, motherhood, communal living, school, and work, wept out of me. Mercifully, the stiff-necked pride with which I'd departed Ceylon melted with tears of humility and forgiveness, and I found myself calling out for help.

Suddenly and most abruptly, I found myself at the cold, metal refrigerator door, which was oddly not unlike hitting the wall of my own ignorance. Brought up short like this, trickles of Bawa's words began to seep into me. Wasn't this child an emissary, come to shake the tree of doubt and confirm the need for trust in the unseen?

Sobered by this wisdom, I collected myself and returned to the unit with my little friend. Kneeling next to his grandmother, I placed the child gently in her arms and whispered softly so that only she could hear, "I know this is hard for you too, but your daughter needs you now. You need to be strong for her. If it's okay with you, I'd like to suggest something—a notion you can choose to believe or not; but if chosen—a notion, that could bring each of you a little peace and comfort." I whispered the words of wisdom that only faith could choose and quietly stepped away and left her to discover and hear her own message from this child-emissary.

This ambassador of light had come for me as well, had come to encourage me to bury pride and arrogance. Tears of humility and forgiveness softened my heart so I could receive the words of comfort and wisdom Bawa continues to send remotely; for indeed, he had not forsaken me. It was I who, in my pride, had let go his hand.

And as if to reward my hard work, after his return to the States, Bawa never once referred to any of these naming shenanigans. He never once addressed me by any of these names. Rather, he started calling me Roser, the name he called my husband, Rodger, and grinning would ask me, "And what kind of rose are you today? Are you a white rose, a yellow rose, or a pink rose?" Playfully, he called me to a higher octave, whereby he encouraged me to sheath the thorns of my karma and to emit the sweet fragrance of God's qualities.

Drowning Kitty Moments

It was early morning, and I had just finished my kitchen duties in the first-floor kitchen. My arms were sore from scrubbing twenty-gallon cooking pots and from kneading mounds of dough—enough for thirty loaves of whole wheat bread. I came into Bawa's room hoping for a rest, but there was a lot of hubbub going on. Bawa was sitting cross-legged on the bed, facing the door. There was a mound of what looked like jewelry piled in front of him. Kathy and a few other room girls were milling around the bed, chattering excitedly. Najma, Dr. Farzad, and Meera wandered in and out of the room from time to time, adding their two cents.

I squeezed in behind the bed and sat with my back to the wall and faced Bawa in front of me. I felt safe in my secluded perch. From here, I could observe the goings on without getting caught in the mêlée. I sat there unwinding from all my business and half-heartedly tried to make sense out the scene before me. Bawa leaned over and picked up one of the objects from the pile, and I could see that it was some kind of silver pendant with Arabic calligraphy. My hearing jumped from voice to voice among the crowd, trying to grasp and piece together the snippets of English or bits of Tamil I might know. From my patchwork listening, I began to get the drift. It seemed I had entered into a brainstorming session about fellowship fundraising. Someone had brought these pendants to Bawa, and I was overhearing a discussion about selling them as a fundraiser.

I sat there detached and watched all the proceedings indifferently, foolishly thinking it had nothing to do with me. But all of a sudden, Bawa turned to me and handed me some of the pendants, giving me instructions. Apparently I was to sell these ten pendants for one hundred dollars apiece. The proceeds were to go to a publishing project. The catch, however, was that I was to pay for the pendants up front. Suddenly, I couldn't breathe. *A thousand dollars!* my mind shrieked. *Yikes!* How was I to ask Rodger, my husband, for a thousand dollars? We were recovering hippies, as you recall. I was in nursing school and working part-time as a nurse's aide, earning $2.60 an hour, and Rodger was working in retail. A thousand dollars was big money for us. I sat there stunned and watched in shock as Bawa called everyone forward and handed them packets of pendants and gave them each the same instructions.

The clouds of shock started to part as I realized I'd better mobilize. I thought to myself selfishly, *Holy moly! He's giving these to everyone! I better get on the stick quick and unload these before the market's flooded and I'm stuck with them!* I snuck from behind the bed and rushed home to the carriage house to make my sales calls. I thought to myself, *I am so clever. I'll call branch members, who live out of town.* I spent the next few hours calling members of the different branches. I called Iowa, California, and Toronto. Time zones complicated my telethon, as many were still sleeping, while others were at work and others were just not available. But over the next few hours, I was able to connect with enough individuals, who were thrilled to receive news from one of their siblings in Philadelphia. "Bawa's doing what? Fundraising? Selling pendants! Yes, of course, I want one!"

So later in the evening, feeling rather smug at my success, I eased back into the room and took up roost again behind the bed. To my horror, there were more pendants. Holy Mary Mother of God, there were more! Hundreds! One of the room girls was kneeling to Bawa's left, sorting the pendants into piles of ten. Another to his right, pen and paper in hand, was keeping accounts. I was in a mental panic, taking this all in. I didn't have any more potential buyers! This was awful!

I had not said anything, mind you. But Bawa, not missing a beat, had sensed my mental hissy fit and had stopped what he was doing and turned to me. He was talking to me, scolding more likely by his tone. I could not make out what he was saying because it was not being translated, but I could tell it was a thrashing, nonetheless. Accounting stopped, and all eyes were on me. I began to make out what he was saying. "Child, a cat licks itself to get clean. If it jumps into the pond, it will drown. Like that, take care of what is yours and leave the rest!" Quickly, he returned to his accounting, and I settled back against the wall to take in this drowning kitty thing.

I ruminated over all the many times I felt likely to drown in the rising emotional tide of being overwhelmed—times, for instance, like those at work when yet another patient was admitted and I burdened myself with the thought of his or her needs, before he or she had even been assigned to me. Or times when I was watching the evening news and I plunged headlong into the troubled waters of the many, ongoing, distant wars—Ethiopia, Syria, Bangladesh, Crimea, or Israel-Palestine—when I hadn't even begun to negotiate peace in my own family and my own community. Indeed, it seemed this kitty needed to *know* her own business and to *mind* her own business. It seemed this kitty needed to focus on cleaning up her own act, before considering the big plunge into depths outside her league.

Drowning Kitty Moments

Getting Old

I came home from work one day, and I was feeling rather sucked dry. I had just spent a grueling week of twelve-hour shifts in the hospital. I could still hear the voice of one of my octogenarian patients. As I walked into Dorothy's room early that morning, she snapped, "Now listen, young lady, if one more do-gooder comes in here and tells me that God doesn't give you more than you can bear, I think I'll just spit on 'em! They just don't know!" I was thinking that if I were to be helpful to my patients, I really need Bawa's help.

After a shower and a cup of tea, I made my way over to Bawa's room and settled into the safety behind his bed and waited for him to reincorporate. I use the expression *reincorporate* because whenever Bawa lay down for meditation, he just felt so *gone*. Mostly, those meditation-sojourns to other realms or dimensions remained a mystery. However, ever so rarely, he would relate snippets from one of those missions. Once I recall his telling us about fighting demons while riding a motorcycle with Michelle, seated on the back. Go figure. Bawa on a motorcycle! While just days before, he had one of the room girls read a letter to those of us sitting in the room from a disciple in Sri Lanka. In the letter, the gentleman related a recent encounter where he spoke with Bawa face-to-face in the streets of Jaffna, only to discover that Bawa was physically in the States at the time.

While I waited for Bawa to come out of his mediation, I pondered. At this point in time, Kubler Ross had surpassed Ms. Clara Barton as my idol, and I had been mentally sorting my patients into Kubler Ross's DABDA groups: the deniers, the angry, the bargainers, the depressed, and the acceptors. The acceptors didn't pose a problem as such for me, but the other three groups pushed the envelope of patience for this little grasshopper, who up till now had personally suffered nothing more serious than a sore throat or a toothache. I had to admit that in my youth and inexperience, I was more than a little self-righteous and thought that most of my patients needed to get a grip and stare this "death thing" in the face. In my naiveté, I thought, *Geez! Bawa has been talking to us about dying before death. Certainly, there must be something I might say to all these individuals to help hasten their surrender!*

While I was lost in thought, Bawa had gotten up and sat quietly, cross-legged on the bed. Auntie Noor, steadfast and patient, stood sentinel at the bedside with a cup of barley water. I waited. Auntie Noor waited. After what felt like forever, Bawa leaned over to me and said, *"Enna? What is it?"* Timidly I brought up the subject of my patients and how to counsel them. I was fully expecting to hear Bawa say, *"Sābur, Shākur, Tawakkul 'allāh, Alhamdu lillāh,"*[16] an expression he repeated with great frequency as he considered the qualities of patience and trust that it expressed, prerequisite to formulating a state of peace. He actually startled me by leaning way over the side of the bed and planting his face close to mine. Looking directly into my eyes, he repeated slowly and deliberately, three times, "Child, getting old is *very* difficult!" He remained there for a moment, looking into my eyes, to make sure I understood. Message delivered, he turned his attention to Auntie Noor and the barley water. Needless to say, I was speechless. I sat back against the wall and thought to myself, *Dana, just be kind. Just be kind. There are no words. Trust kindness to be enough.*

---

[16] *Sābur, Shākur, Tawakkul 'allāh, Alhamdu lillāh* (A): Phrase meaning patience, contentment, trust in God, and giving all praise to God.

22

Shotguns

Midafternoon one day in Ceylon, I wandered into Bawa's room. Oddly, it was very quiet. I remember wondering, "Where is everyone?" the ever-present squawking of crows sounding exceptionally loud in the hollow emptiness of the smooth, cement-walled room. I startled momentarily, as I realized that Bawa was scolding me—no, too strong a word, admonishing me. I took my eyes off him for a moment and looked around, hoping that those words were meant for someone else. But lo, wonder of wonders! It was one of those rarest of moments of aloneness with the sheikh. "You know, child. Words spoken with anger and haste are like shooting someone with a rifle. When the bullet goes in, it makes a small hole, but when it comes out the other side, it makes a big hole."

I knelt there in front of him, flushed and ashamed, as vignettes of painful exchanges between my husband, Rodger, and myself flashed through my mind. I knelt there thinking about all the times I struggled to "speak my truth" to Rodger in what I thought was a simple and direct manner, only to watch the emotional chasm between us widen.

I had never seen a gunshot wound. But later that night while watching television in Bawa's room, almost on cue, a crime scene investigation caught my attention on the TV. I watched as the detective walked over to the prone body, squatted down, and explored a diminutive, clean hole, penetrating the victim's forehead. I watched as he turned the body over to expose the gaping hole in the man's skull, leaking away the man's vitality.

Horrified, I understood what Bawa was trying to tell me. For the first time, I was momentarily able to experience, to really hear and receive my words as others perceived them. Shocked and appalled, I realized that what I thought was just a little thing, just my trying to be frank and forthright, zinged into Rodger like a stealth weapon, entered his mind, and detonated like an IED and blasted a hole in our trust. I sat there, devastated, and thought about all our stored-up goodness—goodness we had assiduously gathered together through the many trials of parenting and forging financial stability in the world. We had stored that goodness in the bund of our shared hearts, only to see it leak out through the holes created by those hasty, careless words. For the first time, I realized how puny words like "I'm sorry" were to patch the hole in that trust. Puny! Like expecting a finger to dam a breach in a water-swollen levy. For the first time, I understand my husband's subtle but distinct, inch-by-inch nightly retreat farther away in the bed, and by day his retreat into superficial pleasantries and the withholding of warmth. For the first time, I saw my part in all this. For the first time, the finger of blame pointed unequivocally at me.

Shot Guns

Misers and a Skunk Doesn't Know Its Own Smell

A central theme to Bawa's spiritual ideology was to "consider the hunger of another as one's own." Ever the teacher, Bawa went to great lengths to demonstrate this lofty code of ethics. For example, in the early 1940s, using only a machete, Bawa cleared eleven acres of scrub forest in the Kilinochchi District of northern Sri Lanka. He cultivated the land and used the proceeds to feed the poor. Later, he gave the farm to his driver to continue overseeing its operation and then started another farm at Pulyankulum. Here he grew produce such as rice, chili peppers, sesame seeds, mangos, bananas, manioc—again, to feed the poor.

Once a year in Jaffna, he orchestrated a massive festival where he fed all who came, without discrimination. Throngs of visitors, rich as well as poor, from each of the four major religions: Christians, Hindus, Buddhists, and Muslims attended. They arrived by foot, by cart, and by auto from all the outlying villages to hear this holy man sing songs of God and to receive their free offerings. Bawa personally attended the vast cauldrons of curry, which were cooked over an open fire. Throughout the day and long into the night, as the myriads arrived, he saw that each attendee received their banana leaf platter of curry and their pennies wrapped in brightly colored papers.

Bawa Inspecting the Farm in Sri Lanka

Bawa continued this practice in the United States. By the early 1980s, the fellowship had purchased one hundred acres of rich farmland in East

Fallowfield, Pennsylvania, near Coatesville. Here under Bawa's direction, we grew truckloads of pumpkins, melons, tomatoes, peppers, and mung beans. Ugh! The mung beans! All those gazillions of tiny seeds had to be freed from their pods and more importantly be accounted for. At any rate, harvest time in Bawa's room looked not unlike the Italian market with sacks of produce piled around his bed. I remember one such occasion.

I entered the room, which was noisy and bustling. I couldn't quite tell what was going on. Someone shoved me into a line and told me that Bawa was selling farm produce. I could see Bawa on his bed, surrounded by what appeared to be a bumper crop of cantaloupe. Someone to his right was keeping accounts of sales, while someone to his left bagged the produce for each buyer.

As I waited my turn, my mind wound into action. *Geez!* I wondered. *There's a lot of melons! Why'd they grow so many? Boy! They certainly didn't pre-pave the distribution aspect of this agricultural venture, did they?* I know! I know! None of my business. Someone from behind nudged me forward. As I inched forward, my mind continued its spin. Let's see. My family lives in the carriage house with two other families. We all share one refrigerator, and I have only one shelf on the bottom of the fridge. My husband and my son don't particularly like melon. So that means I should probably only get one small one. With those thoughts in mind, I eyed a particularly diminutive cantaloupe off to the side.

I was startled from my reverie. Bawa was saying something to me. It sounded like *kanjan* or something. I asked Christine, who was translating, to tell me what he had just said.

"You don't wanna know," she said.

"Come on," I hissed at her under my breath. "Tell me!"

"Trust me," she whispered, "you don't wanna know. Just move on."

By now Bawa had repeated this *kanjan*-thing several times, so I continued to press Christine to translate.

"Okay! Okay!" she said reluctantly. "He just called you a miser."

Someone handed me my wee melon, and mortified, I moved off to the far side of the room to contemplate my new handle. Miser! The *Qutb* of the universe has just called me a miser! As I replayed the reels of my mind and witnessed them from Bawa's perspective, I grudgingly acknowledged my petty, small-mindedness. Not once had I entertained generous thoughts. Not once did I think, *Gee! Bawa's trying to raise money for the fellowship. I could buy lots of these melons. I could share them in the public kitchen downstairs, or take them to work, or donate them to a soup kitchen.*

Perhaps I had managed to hide my karmic pettiness and self-business from the throngs in Bawa's room, but the guru had effortlessly read my mind and mirrored its flaws. Bawa often used the phrase, "A skunk doesn't know its own smell," and indeed, this skunk was oblivious to its selfish stench.

Thirty years later, this interaction still feeds me as I fundraise for my community. Sometimes I am humbled by some donors' openhanded generosity, and at other times I cringe as others, like myself, try to excuse their niggardliness. A refrain from a ditty that Bawa used to sing from time to time plays through my head, "Be like me! Be like me! My Father said to be like He is—so very loving, so very gentle, so very wise." Ach! There's the rub! How to become like this representative of the divine, this wee saint of a man?

Farm Produce in Bawa's Room

Speak the Truth with Patience and World Peace

I n contrast to Bawa's stellar and impeccable clarity, life among the house residents felt more like living in a mental institution. Each of us had come searching relief from our karmic madness and foibles, and I personally felt like I was constantly bumping up against someone by virtue of my own lunacy. One such incident happened while baking a cake in the carriage house one afternoon.

As I said, I was baking a cake. I had intentionally planned my baking, so as to avoid high-traffic times, as there were three women who shared the thirteen-inch, corner-mounted stove on which to feed their respective families. My cake was in the oven, and I was washing the dishes. Out of the corner of my eye, I noticed that one of the other ladies, whom I lived with, was opening the oven door. Shocked that my cake might fall, I spun around and gave her a look, to which she replied, "Don't roll your eyes at me like that!"

Suddenly, I was nine years old again and could hear my mother saying, "Don't you roll your eyes at me like that, young lady!" Words were always so hard with this powerful, Southern belle, who at the age of twenty-three became the first woman lawyer to argue a case against the Supreme Court of South Carolina—and win. So deft with words was this "fair Portia," as the court dubbed her, that she could make black look white. There was no winning with her silver tongue, which could talk any falsehood into truth, but my "bullshit detector" knew differently. Rather than risk sparring with her in the debate ring, my thwarted individualism hopelessly sought expression in frustrated "tudes" of eyeball rolling, saucy hips, and hand gestures. Unwittingly and unbeknownst to me, these ineffective means of expression had followed me into my adulthood.

Over the next few days, I pondered this sublimation of expression into body language. I began to see a pattern in which I dumped into some kind of submissive, passive-aggressive state when I interacted with those whom I felt threatening. I noticed that it was often authority figures. I replayed every tweaky situation in my head but could not come up with an alternative to my habitual behaviors, which apparently did not work. Stumped, I decided to go ask Bawa.

I trotted myself over to Bawa's room. It was as though the seas had parted and I was able to march right up to the bed. Quickly, so as not to lose my gumption, I launched in with, "Bawa, I need to understand something. It seems that I don't always speak my true feelings." As I waited for his reply, I thought to myself, *Well, at least he won't scold me for speaking hastily or arguing or fighting.*

Then I heard him say, *"Periya, periya, pāvum dan!"* Even I didn't need a translator to understand those words. "This is a huge sin or fault!" he said.

Frantically, I started my wagering. *Wait a minute! Just wait a minute! I* thought to myself. *What I just said couldn't have gotten translated correctly. The translator doesn't know what I meant. This isn't what job I should get or which house I should buy. This is psychology, and the Ceylonese translators don't do psychology.* I snuck a look out of the corner of my eye and took note that it was Zara who was translating. Squirming, I thought, *Dang! Zara knows what I meant. She's been educated here in the States and has lived here for ages. My statement got translated correctly all right.* Bawa leaned over and said to me, "Learn to speak the truth with patience—or flush it in the toilet."

I sat there by the side of the bed mentally squirming. I remembered all the times I was engaged in one of those interpersonal, push-pull power struggles, in which I found my sense of equality being run into the ground and my emotional gauge ratcheting toward eruption and would think to myself, *I'll talk about this later when I'm calmer.* But when later came, I'd think, *No. Not now. Not now. Things are goin' too good right now, and I don't wanna blow it.* As time, faithful to its progressive tick and tock, nudged into the future with no arbitration, another offense would hit me in the face, and unable to dodge it, I'd verbally lose it with all the pent-up fury and frustration of unspoken, past history.

Bawa leaned over and interrupted my reverie. "That's exactly what I'm talking about. Learn to speak the truth with patience. Or flush it in the toilet."

Stunned, I backed out of the room to contemplate and unpack the importance of this instruction. Mercifully alone for a moment in my room at the carriage house, I began to grock the magnitude of this offering for the establishment of both personal as well as world peace. I understood how the voiceless thought it plausible to grab, sneak, steal, or otherwise manipulate to get what they wanted or needed, unwittingly fostering disharmony and mistrust. Unfortunately, I was not alone in this inability to speak, nor immune to its consequences. I noted how nations and tribes, worldwide, likewise passive-aggressively overrode boundaries and dropped bombs to satisfy their personal needs.

As I sat, stewing in my own turmoil, the cauldron of world politics boiled with Russia's invasion of Afghanistan and military coups in Grenada, Ghana, and El Salvador, spiced with the pepper of the Iran hostage crisis.

Sitting there, I understood how utterly essential was the diplomacy of this "speak-the-truth-with-patience" business. Oh, how many wars could we prevent if we could just keep people talking. "Wait a minute! Wait a minute! Don't throw that bomb! Talk to me! Talk to me! What do you need?"

I understood how utterly profound was the laying down of one's arms and sitting defenseless and vulnerable before one's foe to smoke the peace pipe and state one's case, for only equals can sit together weaponless. And only in equality can we formulate peace.

✳

Departures

The snowbell tree has finally yellowed
And leaves drop wistfully,
Reminding me of departing souls,
Gentling out of this density to subtler realms,
Reminding me that time is defined
And causing me to question whether I have regrets.
Are there those I have not forgiven
And others to whom my love lies hidden?
I recall all those deep and intimate thoughts
Held secret in my heart,
Which from time to time risk emancipation
And flutter up to freedom,
But like some offending fish bone
Wedge themselves sideways in my throat,
Never to experience the freedom of expression
And the possibility of love.
Will I carry all these pleas for love to grave
As do so many whose deathbed I attend?

The Mosque of His Holiness M.R. Bawa Muhaiyaddeen

Philadelphia, Pa.

25

The Mosque

In 1984, Bawa built a mosque. In the backyard, no less. This just about undid me and my relationship with him. It seemed to me that most of my friends just hopped right on that bus without question. But boy! I was a boiling mess inside! What was he doing? I'd already gone through religion! I'd genuflected, fasted, self-flagellated, and recited obediently for almost two decades without enlightenment. Hadn't I met him after returning from Jerusalem with lesson number two safely in my pocket—God is in the heart, not in a place? Was he asking me to go backward?

I watched in horror as backhoes tore down the trees, uprooted the vegetable garden, ripped out the rose bushes, and swept away the herb beds, from which we made medicinal potions ever so often. I have olfactory memories as pineapple mint, pennyroyal, catmint, basil mint, and of course, spearmint and peppermint released their precious vapors as they fell to the crush and rumble of change.

From start to finish, construction of the mosque took about six months. Daily, Bawa sat perched in his chair in the second-floor landing, monitoring the site below, walkie-talkie in hand. Though disturbed, I still didn't want to be left out, so I joined the ranks of unskilled laborers, who worked collectively to help build this structure—not unlike farmhands at an Amish barn raising. We hauled bricks and stirred cement alongside fine craftsmen such as the bearded letter-cutter and calligrapher, imported from Egypt, who meticulously etched and carved serpentine Arabic letters into the building's marble façade. (Unfortunately, this fellow had to be sent home in disgrace, as he was hugely tempted by the presence of Western women, not covered from head to toe.) Howard Lord Napier, alias Gold-Leaf Howard (another Bawa nickname), followed close behind, crawling along the scaffolding, pressing sheets of twenty-three carat gold leaf into the cursive crevices. Distracted as I was by the buzz and bustle of construction, the full impact of what was to come didn't hit me until after the opening and dedication of the mosque.

I remember the first morning after the dedication. I trotted myself over to Bawa's room and took up my post as usual. All was fine and dandy until about noon, when *Allahu Akbar* came trumpeting over the house speakers. On cue, the other girls obediently rose and drifted off for ablutions and prayers. Not me. I sat there freaking out, hoping that Bawa wouldn't command me to "get along" as he had the other stragglers. This pattern continued daily, with me trying to disappear without disappearing each time the call to prayer came.

Then after a few weeks, when this five-times prayer thing had become a kind of group norm, ever so masterfully, Bawa started stirring the pot. One morning, before the morning session formalized, a group of individuals chatted among themselves at the foot of Bawa's bed about their conversion to Islam and boasted about their observance of the five-times prayers.

"Oh!" said Bawa. "You think all that bending and bowing constitutes prayer? Ha! It should be so easy! True prayer is to remember God with every breath—43, 242 times a day. Besides, there isn't a Muslim in this room! The only true Muslims are babies. You see, only babies love unconditionally. Only babies trust and surrender most totally and never worry about their next meal or whether harm might come to them."

This was music to my ears, but I was still confused and secretly thought Bawa might be waxing a bit poetically, that is until my Syrian friend corroborated this interpretation grammatically. "See here," he said as he flipped through Hans Wehr's *Dictionary of Modern Written Arabic*. "*Islam* comes from the fourth form of the verb, which means 'to hand over or surrender,' and when you add the prefix *mu* to the front of a word, it means 'one who.' Hence, a *Muslim* quite literally means 'one who has surrender to the will of God.'"

Bawa was so clever. He never did shoo me off to the mosque as he did others. Day after day, that call to prayer would come, and I'd sit in his room unmoving, pretending ignorance. And night after night, he would discourse about Muhammad and his tribe. This went on for weeks until one day I thought to myself, *Gee! he hasn't* made *me. Couldn't I just try this out of love for him?*

As it happened, love called me to the mosque, called me to prayer. And miraculously, from time to time, those outer prayers were punctuated with the most brilliant God moments and rhapsody. Those moments might occur quite unexpectedly, such as the morning pride vacated my heart most totally the instant my head touched the ground in prostration—a position, symbolic of complete subservience to the Absolute. For the briefest of moments, pride vacated, leaving humility to swell and soften the heart.

At other moments, contemplation might reveal the tasty fruit of understanding as I butted up against the dry crust of now. I recall one such morning, sitting in the mosque about four in the morning. We were reciting the *Asmā'ul Husnā*. The practice was to recite the names or attributes of Allah out loud in cycles of thirty-three, ninety-nine, and so on with the hopes of revealing an atom of understanding. I was chanting along with the rest of the congregation in this rhythmic, meaningless-to-me monotone. *"Yā Kābìr. Yā Kābìr. Yā* Kābìr."[17] In my typical rebellious

---

[17] *Yā Kābìr* (A): Literally, the Great. The might and power of God.

manner, I thought to myself, So? *So? What does this* Kābìr *mean? What is this greatness of God that Muslims around the world shout with such conviction?* And as I demanded understanding, somehow a shattering occurred. An otherworldly, vibratory pulse, replete with consciousness, enveloped me inwardly and outwardly with the most magnanimous forgiveness, spawned from pure love, a forgiveness big enough, vast enough to forgive all human atrocities, both large and small. And in that moment, for just a moment, I found myself both the object of, as well as the source of that love and forgiveness. And in that moment, I understood the greatness of that forgiveness that, if fostered, could put stop to all wars.

Oh, I hungered for those morsels of bliss and threw myself into this outer form. I didn't realize at the time that this master had set me on a journey to uproot and expose the vast inner realms of hidden and unconscious, inherited ignorance, which covered the light of truth. For the next decade and a half, I became a fanatic in every sense of the word. My head scarf pretty much came off only in the shower, and with my *perpetual prayer schedule* in hand, I adjusted rising for *fajr*, the dawn prayers, by the minute from April's earliest rising at 3:20 a.m. to January's almost decadent and forgiving 5:45. I scrupulously examined every food label for trace of swine and studied Arabic in university, priding myself on reading and reciting the Qur'an, and traveled to Saudi, where I joined the millions in Mecca, circumambulating the Kaaba, for both *hajj*[18] and *umrah.*[19] Fasting became a way to surreptitiously satisfy my anorexic tendencies such that in addition to the month of Ramadan, I was starving myself for all the wrong reasons every voluntary fast day.

I continued in this now-flagrant fanaticism, blindly offending family and friends until I hit a wall—a loveless wall. Foolishly I boo-hoo'ed inwardly about the loss of intimacy in my life. Why, if I was so devout, was there so little love in my life? What had happened to the relationship with my precious firstborn son? Where was that tender mommy love that he had showered on me unquestioningly as a toddler? I was so totally blind to how I had made that child jig to my jog all those years living under my roof until he could make his escape! Blind to all those years that I had *made* him get up for prayers, stripping him of choice. Oh, I was so blind to the expression of arrogance and fanaticism laid down genetically in my blood by the ignorance of my ancestry. This was what Bawa called "blood ties"— those karmic, inherited patterns, those base pairs, passed down generation after generation. Often, he spoke about karma and about how

---

[18] *Hajj* (A): The prescribed pilgrimage to the holy city of Mecca that takes place in the last month of the year that all Muslims are expected to make once in their lifetime.

[19] U*mrah* (A): The lesser pilgrimage made by Muslims, which may be performed at any time of year.

it was almost impossible to crack the code and break their stranglehold without the wisdom and guidance of a true *gnāna sheikh*,[20] a real guru.

And to think that it was through the mosque that Bawa had exposed this sin of fanaticism and its cousins, pride and egoism. Unfortunately, the whole world is just about as ignorant as I and continues even today to fight its religious wars, ignorantly supposing that the enemy is out there. Islam is not the sin, nor is any other religion. No, it is this sword of pride of fanaticism, "I know! I'm right! I, I, I!" that beheads the other.

It was for this that the guru came. He came to lead the way out of darkness, to awaken within us the station of wisdom by which we might navigate home. He came as the mirror to expose the dross that we might choose light, for only purity can know purity.

And no, I don't cover my head anymore and have "gone underground" and blend with the rest of my neighbors in my suburban community. From here I continue this work of purification, recalling Bawa's words, "A true Sufi cannot be known by his dress, rather by his qualities and actions."

The Call to Prayer

In the quiet,
In the dawn,
The call does come.

---

[20] *Gnāna Sheikh* (T and A): Teacher; a gnostic with divine wisdom.

Like some silvery-throated thrush,
It calls to me.
"Wake up! Wake up!
Come!" It calls.
"Come to prayer."

And further does the call command,
"Wash hand and foot and mind and heart.
Join sister, brother, friend, and foe.
Stand side by side in measured rows
Like silent trees that wait a cleansing wind.

"And when the wind of grace does blow,
Together bow before your Lord.
Place face to floor and heart to ground,
And thus humbled,
Find
Freedom
In
Forgiveness."

26

The Washer of Teacups

One afternoon, I was sitting in the car with my friend Daniel. Daniel was in charge of the Publishing Department and was essentially my boss in the office where I transcribed Bawa's discourses. We had just run errands together and before our good-byes, were having one of those delicious sharing sessions, recalling poignant moments with the sheikh.

Daniel was telling me about the time Bawa charged him with the duty of preparing a presentation with regard to the Publishing Department and its progress. Orders received, Daniel left Bawa's room and went off to his office, where he got out pen and paper. Over the next few hours, he laboriously and meticulously drew charts and spreadsheets, outlining the nitty-gritty of Bawa's words from first utterance to "hot off the press." Carefully, he traced the pathway from translators to transcribers, proofreaders, English editors, Tamil editors, printers, binders, collators, and such. He carefully noted each individual's name and job description. He gave them each a title and plugged them into the master plan next to their respective duties. Satisfied that he had completed his mission, he returned to Bawa.

Back in Bawa's room, before Daniel could even whip out his handiwork, Bawa proceeded to tell him down to the minutest details the content of the documents. Puzzled, Daniel thought to himself, *Okay, now what's going on? Why did he have me do this if he already knew everything?* Still not missing a beat, Bawa said, "You know, *Tambi*, you only made one mistake. But it's a very big mistake—one little but very big mistake. You gave everyone a title." Daniel was even more puzzled now.

Bawa grinned and reached down and picked up his teacup from the bedside table. "You see this teacup, *Tambi?* It's dirty. It needs to be washed. Now if you wash this teacup, do you become 'the washer of the teacup'?" Blank stare from Daniel. Bawa leaned closer. "Or if I have ten dirty teacups, do you become 'the washer of teacups?' Grinning, Bawa leaned in even closer, almost face-to-face. "And if I have fifty dirty cups, are you 'the master washer of the teacups'? Or if I have a hundred cups, are you 'the grand master washer of the teacups?' *Tambi*, there is only the needing to be washed and the washing. Do you understand?"

Sitting in the backseat of the car, listening to Daniel tell this story, my mind exploded as I began to get the simplicity of Bawa's illustration. For a moment, I understood that there is only this isness, this movement, this power, this current of life, this God energy that permeates all, knows all, loves all, creates, nourishes, and sustains, does all this in a complete state of purity or innocence, with no sense of self. As soon as an "I-label" is applied, the grandest identity crisis of all occurs. Otherness happens, separation occurs, as though one has "stepped outside the flow" and one becomes the observer of the flow, but is not the flow. And from this one very little but very big mistake, from this one little "I" thought, all suffering occurs. All suffering occurs from this misidentification as the washer of cups.

For a moment, I imagined my toddler son. I witnessed how this current flowed through his tiny being and how he beamed toothless with delight and how he rode the current without sense of self. As he rode the flow, there was no sense of lack, no doubt, no fear, no need. He was the joy. He was the contentment. He was the trust.

Sitting there in the backseat of the car, I recalled how Bawa also talked about what he called the graft. He talked about how the soul was pure, innocent, and fully aware of its source. He explained that during that soul's sojourn in the world, teachers, parents, religious leaders, friends, and well-wishers graft onto that soul all their perceived truths until ultimately that soul forgets its true nature. Bawa explained that it is paramount for each individual to develop wisdom, for it is wisdom that can cut off all these grafts. He explained that in order to end suffering and to know peace, it was essential, using one's wisdom, to cut off all these washer of cups identities so that one could reclaim the true rootstock of one's being.

Buried Treasure—
West Park Hospital

In the summer of 1986, Bawa's health deteriorated to the point that he was rushed to West Park Hospital nearby, where one of the fellowship doctors had admitting privileges. Unable to breathe on his own, he was admitted into the intensive care unit and placed on a respirator. Visitors were restricted to the doctors and a handful of Ceylonese followers and translators, who kept twenty-four-hour vigils in shifts.

One afternoon during this period, Auntie Noor asked me to drive her over to the hospital, as it was her turn to sit with Bawa. Needless to say, I was thrilled to be of service. So I packed Auntie Noor into my car, along with all her requisite vigil-vittles and necessities: one thermos of warm water (the imbibing of cold liquids being strictly verboten to the Ceylonese); an even larger forty-ounce thermos of spiced, sweet tea; one three-tiered, stainless steel tiffin, food carrier, filled with curries; one well-worn Qur'an and prayer shawl; and yes, even in July, a wool sweater. As she left me standing in the hallway, outside Bawa's curtained cubby, Auntie Noor instructed me, "Now, darling, you just wait outside here. Someone will be going back with you to the Fellowship House." Thus instructed, I stood outside Bawa's cubby and waited in the hallway. After about fifteen minutes or so of waiting, I started to get antsy and started to pace. Up, down. Up, down. I paced back and forth the length of the sterile hallway.

After what felt like an eternity, the curtain whipped open, and someone grabbed me by the arm and pulled me into the cubby. Dr. Farzad, Auntie Noor, and Dr. Kumar were all shouting at me at once, almost angry. I didn't know what to make of all this high emotion, and most certainly, I could not understand what I might have to do with their distress. Through all the garble, gradually I began to understand the reason for their consternation. I looked down at my dear, sweet Bawa, who had been rendered mechanically mute by the ventilator tube shoved down his throat. His beautiful face was crisscrossed with white strips of paper tape, which anchored the tubing.

It seemed that Bawa had seen my feet as I paced in the hallway. For over fifteen minutes, gagged as he was, with grunts and eyes and hands, he had tried to get them to understand that he wanted to talk to me. "What do you need, Bawangal?" they pleaded. "Are you in pain?" they asked. Over and over, they miserably failed at charades, as he repeatedly gestured to the curtain, "Do you need the doctor? Are you having trouble breathing?" Until finally, someone had the brilliant idea to open the curtain.

I looked down at my beautiful father, and although taped and tubed as he was, his eyes still held their penetrating gaze. With those lasers, he locked eyes with me and then raised his right hand, extending his index finger in a gesture of absoluteness. "One! There is only one!" his eyes commanded. "Know this!" his eyes commanded. And then message delivered, his hand fell limply to the bed and he closed his eyes.

I eased out of the cubby and went to wait in my car for my return passenger. As I waited, I sobbed silently. To see Bawa suffer like this was so very, very hard, but it was also so equally hard to fathom that someone loved me this indisputably and cared for my salvation so profoundly that he did not trust the message to some other envoy but called me to his deathbed and personally bestowed upon me the map to the buried treasure.

28

Passages—Stethoscopes and Heart Connections

Sick as he was, Bawa was still very much in charge and demanded that he be brought home, asserting that he had important spiritual work to complete and that there were far too many distractions in the hospital. The coterie of medical doctors in charge of his care conceded that yes, all the flashing lights, beeps, and buzzers could indeed be disruptive, but concerned for his wellbeing, they continued to argue the necessity of his hospitalization from every angle. However, when Bawa waved off the beeping and buzzing as nonissues and explained that he was kept much too busy exorcizing the hospital of all the many demons that showed up daily to prey on the weak and sick, there was not much they could say. He came home promptly after this discussion—not without major restrictions and cautions, however.

The morning after his return, I was crouched on the far side of Bawa's bed, trying desperately to hide, as one of Bawa's attending physicians was passionately explaining to Bawa that he should not! could not! would not! continue to work at his previous pace and that "*furthermore* only doctors and those immediately necessary to Bawa's care should be allowed into the room. Period! And lest there be any confusion, here is a list of those individuals!" I must have taken a breath or something because I knew I was sitting as motionless as a rabbit confronting a pit bull, when suddenly this doctor noticed me and turned beet-red in exasperation. But before he could oust me, Bawa leaned over, put his hand on my head, and said, "She stays."

Yahoo! I could stay! But like all youth, I was in complete denial that there was a winter to every spring and that this precious being of light was subject to the same elemental laws and terms of agreements as the rest of us mere mortals. You see, in my innocence, I ascribed superman qualities to Bawa and was somewhat oblivious to his human suffering, which now from my backward perch, I can see was monumental.

Nights were raw. Bawa's aged and scarred lungs refused to inflate as he lay prone. So he spent his nights sitting up, hunched over a hospital bed table, tugging at his breathing machine. One of his disciples, an anesthesiologist, had cleverly jury-rigged the machine to operate like a positive-pressure ventilator. He dubbed this confabulation his *supi*, a Tamil word for pacifier, and lightheartedly likened himself to a baby sucking on a pacifier. At any rate, I sat there in attendance through the long nights, watching helplessly as he tugged at that machine for every breath. I can still hear the eerie sound of its rhythmical, mechanical suck and spew.

Most nights, somewhere close to dawn Bawa was finally able to lie down. But not for long. As soon as the early morning prayers ended, petitioners trickled into the room, and like baby birds, flapping and squawking, they demanded sustenance. "Feed me. I'm hungry," they demanded. I remember feeling so utterly outraged by their neediness. But then again, they were oblivious to Bawa's sleepless nights, and I had had the privilege of sitting in his presence.

Always the servant, he fed them. They came from all corners of the world, seeking comfort. Denmark, Istanbul, Texas, Uganda. To a man from the Caribbean, worried about his brother, who practiced Satanism, Bawa suggested the impossible nature of such worship. "Ah, child, how foolish to light candles to Satan. He cannot see the light." To the couple from Uganda, he offered the unity of all humankind, suggesting that all children are children of Adam and that all babies commune with God, that is until parents teach them about the world such that they forget. To the theology students from Villanova and St. Joseph's University, he spoke about sticky social issues such as celibacy, sex, AIDS, and homosexuality. To Coleman Barks, poet and literature professor, he likened writing to farming, suggesting that a writer must plant the right words in the right soil at the right season to make his point clear and ensure a good crop.

Over the next few months, which none of us knew were to be his last, he worked doggedly in between pulls on his *supi*. David Freudberg, a broadcaster from WGBH public radio in Boston, did a series of interviews with Bawa on the true nature of Islam. These became his final book, *Islam and World Peace*. Passionately, Bawa urged each of us to take responsibility for world peace. "This holy war, *jihad*,[21] is not something that can be fought on the outside; our real enemies have been within us. Our own evil qualities are killing us. They are the enemies that must be conquered." [22] In between pulls on his *supi*, he spoke like this. With words of wisdom, he fed each one and stroked each of us into ease, until it all just stopped.

I'll never forget the day Erik and Jackie came to visit. It was after a particularly tough night, and Bawa sat quietly on his bed—just staring. The atmosphere in the room was tender, and somehow those of us sitting around knew not to talk, not to break the silence. Erik and Jackie sat in the corner of the room, their eyes hungry and pleading. Silently, Bawa turned to look at them. He studied them for a bit and then quietly whispered, "I've nothing left to give," and then looked away.

This statement came as a shock, like blowing a fuse during the peak

---

[21] *Jihād* (Arabic): holy war, from the verb to denounce, deny, reject

[22] *Islam and World Peace: Explanations of a Sufi*, p. 2.

performance of a rock concert. Bawa's lights flickered a bit over the next few days and came back to dim but never regained their full wattage. Word went out to the entire community, and the fellowship house filled to maximum capacity as we all held twenty-four-hour vigil. I never left his bedside after that moment. I cannot recall how many days I didn't sleep.

My last memory is a particularly frantic moment when Bawa's doctors and all those in attendance surrounded the bed. I was listening to Bawa's heart with a stethoscope. The doctors were arguing the pros and cons of readmitting him to the ICU to stabilize his taxed breathing. Dr. Petrov, Dr. Susan, Dr. Zurita, Dr. Farzad, Dr. Blunt, Dr. Kumar—the whole lot of them!—stood around frantically arguing! And then his heart stopped. It just stopped. I looked up, and everyone was wildly debating the urgency to do something, anything to stabilize Bawa's condition. But no one—no one but me—new he was gone.

It was surreal. I wormed my way through the throng and shoved the stethoscope toward this gaggle of fine physicians that they might understand the true nature of the moment. Dr. Blunt took the stethoscope from me and listened to Bawa's heart, and the next thing I knew, all the women were asked to leave the room so the men could prepare Bawa's body for burial.

Bawa was gone. Gone? To where? Oh, I struggled over the loss of Bawa's physical form. Oh, indeed, this flower had become so very attached to the tree in hopes of blooming. Life went on. But I was like a dry fish—until the morning two of my girlfriends recounted dreams, in which Bawa had come to them. Oh, I was hurt and angry! I flounced up to the mosque, plopped myself down, and began to hurl angry bullets at God. "Why them and not me? Did Bawa love those girls more? Why hadn't he come to me? Didn't I count!" On and on I railed until I lost all my bluster. And then clear as a bell, Bawa's voice spoke to me. "Child. Where do you think I went? Where did I go?" And in that moment, I recalled standing at the bedside, listening to his heart with the stethoscope, and suddenly I imagined his spirit traveling up that little plastic tube and then settling in my heart. "Yes, that's right. Into your heart."

"But, but, but," I argued. "I can't always hear you so clearly!"

And then he chuckled. "And so what else is new? When I was in the physical from and you asked me a question and I answered, you questioned whether the translators had translated correctly."

And still I wagered, "But why do you come to the others in dreams?"

To which he replied, "Child, forget about the others. Forget about dreams. Trust yourself to go deep into the core of your being past the pull of blood ties, past the wagering of desire, past the ripples of the mind. You *know* me. You know me as well as any mother knows her child. So, *find* me. Find that love. Find that wisdom in the silence of your heart. Sit with me in your heart as you did those many silent nights. Sit with me."

The Compass Rose

For so long, I trusted these physical eyes to chart my homeward journey.
I rocketed through life,
Dazzled and distracted by all the advertisements,
Sampling all the condiments along the way.
But now, blinded by illusion's inexhaustible billboards,
I stand lost among life's thorns,
Weary and exhausted,
Unable to see,
Wanting You.

How to find that distant home,
That place of peace and sweet repose?
Desperate, I recheck the GPS coordinates of my heart.
North by *now* and south by *is*.
Baffled, I wonder how so this dark and scary place my destination be.
But then I catch Your sweet and subtle scent.
For like the gentle rose, You perfume Your presence
So that even sightless, I might find You among the thorns
And continue home.

Conclusion

Years later, long after Bawa's passing, I take out these memories and study them from a new perspective. Here was this fabulously wise being, steadfastly dedicated to establishing world peace, who had worked strategically from the underground for almost a century, yes, one hundred years. He tweaked the minds of individuals like me, as well as the minds of scholars, religious leaders, politicians, and world dignitaries. He adjusted the aperture of our vision to get us to see, really see, that all these billions of souls here on earth were brother and sister, offspring of Adam, genetically bound as one family. He wanted us to know that each and every soul was essential to the body as a whole and that not one of them could be amputated or disregarded without injury to the whole. And for my part, he had given not one but three names with which adjust the aperture of my heart—Ma'rufah, the eternal wisdom that never dies, and Baseerah, the all-seeing one, that sees the within and the without, and Ma'bubah, the all-loving one, who embraces everyone with love.

This tiny, ant man from the jungles of Sri Lanka came for me, came for all of us. He descended into this dark, dense world—this pit of suffering, to guide us home. He came bearing the gift of wisdom so that we might throw off the shackles of our ignorance. He came to open our eyes and point us in the right direction. He also brought the gift of love so we might regain faith in humankind and restore the certainty of returning complete and whole to our origins—that place of divine peace and tranquility